BURBANK

Centennial History
1911–2011

BURBANK

Centennial History

1911–2011

Celebrating Our Past and Embracing Our Future

Burbank City Hall
275 East Olive Avenue
Burbank, CA 91502

Published in cooperation with
Reedy Press
PO Box 5131
St. Louis, MO 63139, USA
www.reedypress.com

Library of Congress Control Number:
2011920039

ISBN: 978-1-935806-00-4

Please visit our website at
www.reedypress.com.

Design by Jill Halpin

Printed in China
11 12 13 14 15   5 4 3 2 1

Acknowledgments

Burbank Centennial History, 1911–2011: Celebrating Our Past and Embracing Our Future represents a collaborative effort that involved an array of resources. We extend our gratitude to the incredibly dedicated researchers and photographers who contributed to this project.

Special thanks to the Burbank Centennial Committees and the Burbank Historical Society.

Contents

Foreword

On some subconscious level a lot of people can't help but imagine that I grew up in the little fictional town of Mayberry, North Carolina. In many ways, my professional life was surely shaped by working on the *Andy Griffith Show*. But my true self, the one that exists in the real world we all share, was influenced by a place, too—a real place—Burbank.

Though my wife Cheryl and I haven't lived in Burbank for decades, family and work bring me "home" many times a year. Every now and then, I take the time to cruise by places that stir memories of my youth. Cordova Street, where my parents, Rance and Jean, settled in 1958, brings a flood of memories. I had my first Halloween on Cordova. Dressed in a suit of cardboard armor made out of boxes and sprayed silver, I experienced the thrill of collecting treats and sharing the excitement with a community of kids. My first lasting friendships were made on that block, as we moved to the corner of Oak and Cordova, where mom and dad bought their first home. I would rush home from the professional make-believe world of Mayberry to the unscripted, unrestrained play world on Cordova with my buddies and our games of army, sports, skateboards, and even a few arguments and bloody noses!

I like to drive by Verdugo Park, Olive Rec, and McCambridge Park and think about all the ups and downs of playing and coaching in the fantastic youth programs of Burbank. The hours and hours of time safely hanging out at Verdugo, working on basketball skills, but really building the life skills of the real world.

And then there is St. Joseph's, where I remember welcoming my brother Clint into our family—the same St. Joseph's where I said a final good-bye to my mother forty-one years later. Behind the hospital is Buena Vista Park (now Johnny Carson Park), where my dad and I took a long walk after my mom's passing. It was soothing to be at that park, because it's a place where we often picnicked, where I directed my first 16 mm short film, and where I courted Cheryl, whom I met in eleventh grade at John Burroughs High School.

Today, I still love to play a round of golf with Clint and my son at DeBell. I still like being surrounded by the studio lots, strolling the friendly neighborhoods, and, most of all, simply recalling what the city has meant to us Howards over these fifty-plus years.

Congratulations Burbank on one hundred beautiful years!

Jean and Rance Howard pose with their sons (from left) Clint and Ron.

Foreword

The happiest years of my life were spent growing up in Burbank. My father, Ray Reynolds, decided to move our family from El Paso, Texas, to Burbank to give us a better life. He built our mother Maxene, my brother Bill, and me a home on Evergreen Street in Magnolia Park through a Federal Housing Agency (FHA) loan.

I attended Roosevelt Elementary School, Burbank High School, and John Burroughs High School. I learned about music, became a member of the band, and a baton twirler.

My life changed in 1948 when I became Miss Burbank, which led to my show business career.

When I was a child, I used to ride my bicycle from our home on Evergreen to the El Portal Theatre on Lankershim Boulevard in North Hollywood to watch movies. To this day, I still perform every year at the El Portal.

Happy one-hundredth birthday wishes to Burbank!

Foreword

Burbank has been my home for more than forty-five years. During that time my wife, Barbara, and I have raised three children, nurtured at least a dozen dogs and cats, and taken the walk down Riverside Drive thousands of times. The neighborhood offers everything we need: good food, smart people, and softball at Izay Park (what I call Olive Park), where I have played for thirteen seasons.

When I opened the doors of the Falcon Theatre in 1997, it was a dream come true. I still proudly display the Falcon championship softball trophies in the lobby. There is nothing I like doing better than meeting-and-greeting the audience before one of our shows. I hope I'm still greeting people at one hundred, when I get to be as old as the city itself.

Thank you Burbank for letting me call you home; thank you for letting me work in your town with the shortest commute to my theatre ever; and thank you for giving me the joy of playing softball as long as my knees hold out. Here's to another one hundred years of joy along Riverside Drive!

BURBANK

Centennial History

1911–2011

Burbank Block, 1911. Photo courtesy of
Burbank Historical Society.

Chapter One

Remembering
Our Past

The Southern California land nestled along the base of the Verdugo Mountains was once homeland for Native American hunters and gatherers. It later evolved into a Spanish Rancho, to a patchwork of American farmland, to a city supporting aerospace, and to the Media Capital of today.

For centuries, the Shoshone-Paiute and Tongva tribes resided in the region near the Verdugo foothills. They hunted small game and gathered acorns from local oak trees. These Native Americans established a vast trade network with tribes that resided along the California coast.

In the 1700s, the Spanish arrived and began settling in the territory. In the late 1700s, the Spanish governor of California awarded land grants to loyal soldiers wishing to retire and settle in the New World. In 1798, one of the largest land grants was awarded to Corporal Jose Maria Verdugo and called the Rancho San Rafael. This land stretched roughly from the Arroyo Seco in present-day Pasadena to the Mission San Fernando. Verdugo built a ranch house, raised cattle, and grew grapes and other crops on the Rancho.

In 1861, Verdugo's children inherited his property. Julio took the southern portion, and Catalina took the northern part of the Rancho. Later, the Verdugos contracted numerous bad debts and eventually sold most of their property.

Jonathan R. Scott was one of the first Americans to purchase a large portion of the Rancho San Rafael. Another land grant, approximately 4,600 acres, was located to the south of Scott's property and was called the Rancho Providencia. This property was purchased by Alexander Bell and David W. Alexander, two Los Angeles City Council members. Scott's portion of the Rancho San Rafael and the Rancho Providencia were later sold to Dr. David Burbank. The combined property would eventually become the town of Burbank.

Dr. Burbank arrived in Los Angeles in 1867 and began buying real estate. With the property purchased from the Ranchos San Rafael and Providencia, he had a substantial land holding. The New Hampshire–born dentist built a ranch house on what is now Warner Bros. Studios, and became one of the most successful sheep ranchers in Southern California.

The Providencia School District was established, and Dr. Burbank donated the land to build the first school on Burbank Boulevard near what is now Mariposa Street.

In the early 1870s, the Southern Pacific Railroad Company began construction on a line to connect Los Angeles and San Fernando. By 1886, train fares were set low to entice people to travel to the Los Angeles area. This ignited a real estate boom. Dr. Burbank sold his Rancho property for $250,000 to a group of land speculators who formed the Providencia Land, Water and Development Company, and he would serve on the Board of Directors.

Top Left: Dr. Burbank's Ranch, 1910.
Top Right: Dr. David Burbank.
Bottom Right: Burbank Train Depot, 1925.
Facing Page, Far Left: Early Burbank area map.
Photos courtesy of Burbank Historical Society.

Top Left: Northeast Burbank, 1908. Photo courtesy of Burbank Historical Society.

Top Right: Providencia Land, Water and Development Company, 1889. Photo courtesy of Burbankia.

Bottom Left: Cantaloupe farm. Photo courtesy of Burbank Historical Society.

The town of Burbank was officially established in 1887 when the Providencia Land, Water and Development Company started selling parcels of the land. The speculators laid out a business district and subdivided the property into small farms and residential lots. By the end of the year, real estate sales amounted to $475,000.

Agriculture and sheep herding became the primary industries of the growing community. This fertile land, much of it fed by natural springs and groundwater, was ideal for farming and ranching. Located approximately halfway between Los Angeles and San Fernando, Burbank farmers produced crops of peaches, grapes, alfalfa, citrus, melons, and other fruits and vegetables. At one time, Burbank produced most of the watermelons and cantaloupes sold in Southern California. Olive groves were planted north of San Fernando Boulevard, and much of the Providencia land was used for sheep and small ranches.

As larger tracts of property were subdivided, farmers moved into the valley region of Burbank. Pioneer families in Burbank such as Fischer, Lutge, Myer, Shelton, Story, Lamer, Peyton, Doan, Forbes, and MacFarlane were well known among the farming community and some were later memorialized by street names in town. As Burbank began to grow, so did the need for services such as banking, town meetings, and postal pick-up.

Top Left: San Fernando Boulevard, 1914.

Top Right: Luttge Brothers' Wagon, 1912.

Bottom: Forsyth Chicken Farm on Magnolia Boulevard, 1903.

Photos courtesy of Burbank Historical Society.

In 1888, construction was completed on the first commercial brick building, "Burbank Block." This building was located on Olive Avenue and San Fernando Boulevard and originally designed to be a bank. Once completed it served as the Burbank Post Office. It housed the library and was also used for religious services and City Trustee meetings. The building was remodeled and rebuilt several times over the years, and many of the decorative elements and Victorian cupola were removed after the 1910 earthquake.

Top: Burbank Block also served as the post office, 1911.

Bottom: Burbank State Bank, 1908, located across the street from the Burbank Block.

Photos courtesy of Burbank Historical Society.

In 1889, Dr. Burbank and his son-in-law, John Griffin, built a picturesque hotel with wide verandas, gables, and turrets, called the Burbank Villa. The structure cost $30,000 to build and was intended to house prospective land buyers. The Burbank Villa was located on Olive Avenue. For a short time, the business prospered but was eventually sold and renamed the Santa Rosa Hotel. This building, later purchased by the U.S. government, was torn down to build a Post Office (current location of Bob Hope Post Office).

Bottom: Burbank Villa Hotel, 1887. Photo courtesy of Burbank Historical Society.

Inset: Burbank Villa Hotel advertisement. Photo courtesy of Burbankia.

In the 1890s, the real estate boom came to a crashing halt, and many real estate speculators faced financial ruin. Despite economic decline, the natural fertility of the surrounding farmland enabled ranchers to survive the lean years. Vineyards flourished, and Burbank became known for producing fine wine. A number of wineries operated in the early 1900s including Randisi, McClure, Brusso, Gai, and Grangetto. The Brusso Winery, located at Thornton Avenue and Ontario Street, survived Prohibition in the 1920s by producing excellent grape juice. It returned to the wine-making business in 1933 until it closed in 1967.

In the early twentieth century, one of Burbank's claims to fame was as the home of James J. Jeffries, the 1899 Heavyweight Boxing Champion of the World. In 1904, Jeffries purchased a 107-acre Burbank ranch located on what is now Buena Vista Street and Victory Boulevard. He grew alfalfa and raised prize-winning cattle on the property. Eventually, Jeffries developed a herd of thoroughbred bulls and began exporting them to Mexico and South America.

Top: McClure Winery. Photo courtesy of Burbank Historical Society.

Middle: Brusso Winery, 1926. Photo courtesy of Burbank Historical Society.

Bottom: Grape Pickers and Queen. Photo courtesy of Jeanette Henderson.

Perhaps his greatest feats were not in the fighting ring but in helping the Burbank community. The Jeffries Barn, located on Victory Boulevard and Buena Vista Street, served as the site for Thursday-night boxing matches and many civic and philanthropic events. The building was later dismantled and placed on exhibit at Knott's Berry Farm. Jeffries was such a beloved figure in the Burbank community that a street was named after him upon his death in 1953.

In 1907, another leading citizen in the community, Dr. Elmer H. Thompson, opened the first hospital in town at the southeast corner of Olive Avenue and Fifth Street. It was named Burbank Community Hospital and in 1990 re-named Thompson Memorial Medical Center after its original founder. It was razed in 2001.

[Incorporation]

In 1911, two significant events affected the future of Burbank—the arrival of the "Red Car" and the incorporation into a city. These events brought business and industry to the small farming community and led to a population boom.

The Pacific Electric Railroad Company completed construction of a streetcar line from Los Angeles to Glendale. Burbank civic leaders approached the company about extending the interurban train line into Burbank. Pacific Electric officials were reluctant due to Burbank's small population. They finally agreed with the stipulation that Burbank subsidize the project. Civic boosters agreed and raised $48,000 by private subscription. A right-of-way was established down Fourth Street (now Glenoaks Boulevard) to Orange Grove Avenue. In 1924, the tracks were extended to Scott Road.

Top: San Fernando Boulevard at Angeleno Street, 1911. Photo courtesy of Burbank Historical Society.

Bottom Left: Pacific Electric "Red Car." Photo courtesy of Burbankia.

Bottom Right: Pacific Electric Station from Fourth Street. Photo courtesy of Burbank Historical Society.

Top: First Burbank City Hall, 1921.

Middle Left: First police car, 1921.

Middle Right: Burbank Fire Department, 1923.

Bottom: Burbank's first mayor, Thomas Story.

Photos courtesy of Burbank Historical Society.

Civic leaders realized that the completion of the train tracks would link Burbank to Los Angeles and surrounding communities and accelerate the town's growth. They decided that they wanted to make Burbank an incorporated city before the arrival of the big "Red Cars."

The population of Burbank was five hundred when the voters approved incorporation on July 8, 1911. A Board of Trustees comprised of F. A. Halburd, Thomas Story, Martin Pupka, J. T. Shelton, and C. J. Forbes was selected to run the City. J. A. Swall was chosen as city clerk and Ralph O. Church, city treasurer. The Board elected Thomas Story as Burbank's first mayor.

The new City government approved a series of infrastructure improvements that included lighting homes and streets with electricity, naming the streets and numbering the houses, expanding the U.S. postal service, establishing city marshals as law enforcement, and building a new grammar school. A bond was passed to improve the water system and build a municipally owned water and power district. By 1916, Burbank had built a new city hall and purchased a fire truck for the volunteer fire department.

The Board of Trustees created the first city seal, depicting a cantaloupe, which represented Burbank's agricultural roots, and credited this melon for getting the town through the lean years following the collapse of the real estate boom.

A festive event was planned and a crowd of nearly one thousand was on hand to welcome the "Red Car." Flags were waving, a brass band playing, and church bells ringing as the streetcar rolled into Burbank. City leaders developed a slogan to market the city: "Burbank – 45 minutes from Broadway."

A leading opponent to incorporation was J. W. Fawkes, a colorful inventor, farmer, and activist. He also proposed to build a monorail from Burbank to Los Angeles. Fawkes called his invention the "Aerial Swallow." City officials, however, called it "Fawkes' Folly," as the proposed monorail system was never completed.

In 1914, Burbank outlawed the manufacturing, transportation, importing, exporting, and sale of alcoholic beverages. Unfortunately, bootlegging became a thriving business. Bootleggers kept marshals and federal agents busy with illegal stills and moonshine distilleries around town.

Beginning in 1917, business and industry began to move into Burbank. Civic leaders Ralph O. Church and Maurice Spazier raised $25,000 and bought Henry Lutge's farm at San Fernando Boulevard and Alameda Avenue. The Lutges, were early Burbank pioneers who owned the general store. Church and Story approached Watt Moreland about relocating his prosperous truck company to Burbank, offering him free land to build his factory. Moreland Motor Truck Company became Burbank's first major industry. For years afterward, the Moreland trucks traveled the highways of the world bearing the label "Made in Burbank." The company closed its doors in 1940 when wartime shortages impacted truck production.

Top: J. W. Fawkes.

Top Right: Pacific Electric Red Car celebration, September 3, 1911.

Bottom Left: Aerial Swallow, "otherwise known as Fawkes' Folly."

Bottom Right: Moreland Motor Truck Company and Grand Opening program, circa 1920.

Photos courtesy of Burbank Historical Society.

SHOOT IF YOU MUST THIS OLD GRAY HEAD
T SPARE YOUR COUNTRY'S FLAG SHE SAID

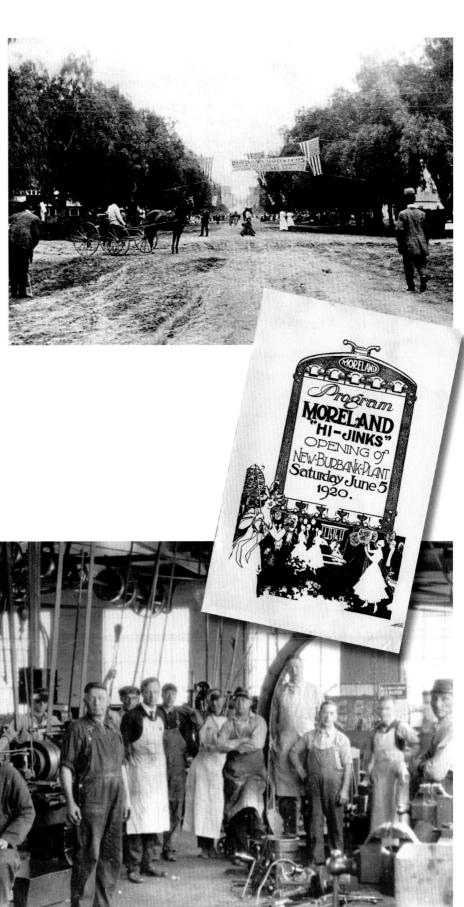

Other companies soon followed Moreland and established factories in Burbank. American Aluminum Corporation, Empire China Company (the future home of Lockheed), the Libby, McNeill & Libby Canning Company, Hinkley Peach Canning Company, and Andrew Jergens Company were among some of the many industries who took advantage of Burbank's ideal location and close proximity to Los Angeles.

Oliver J. Stough was one of the wealthiest landowners in Burbank. He built a sizeable house on Sixth Street between Cornell Drive and Bethany Road. He was the first depositor in the Burbank State Bank with $500, and he contributed $8,000 for the Pacific Electric "Red Car" extension into Burbank. In 1914, at the age of ninety-six, he sold his remaining property in Burbank for $1 million. Stough is best known for the land he deeded to the City that would eventually become Stough Park.

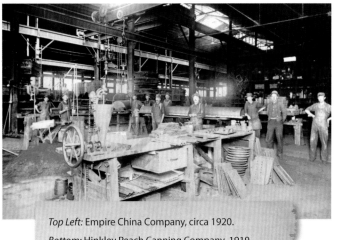

Top Left: Empire China Company, circa 1920.

Bottom: Hinkley Peach Canning Company, 1919.

Photos courtesy of Burbank Historical Society.

Even before the motion picture studios moved into Burbank, residents enjoyed silent picture shows at the Loma Theatre, located on San Fernando Boulevard. The Loma opened in 1919 and was later equipped with the Vitaphone® sound system and billed as "The Best in Talking Pictures." The famed theatre, along with its Sweet Shop, was later damaged during the 1971 Sylmar Earthquake. Several years later it was demolished and is now the location of the Burbank Holiday Inn parking structure.

Top Right: Loma Theatre, San Fernando Boulevard.

Top Left: Oliver J. Stough home on Sixth Street.

Inset left: Oliver J. Stough.

Bottom: Andrew Jergens Company, 1927.

Photos courtesy of Burbank Historical Society.

[Early Real Estate Development]

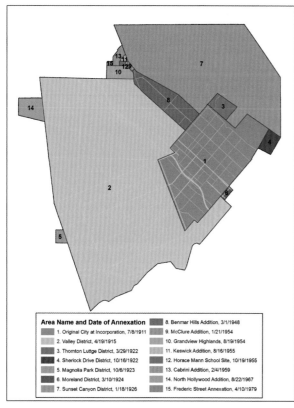

Area Name and Date of Annexation
1. Original City at Incorporation, 7/8/1911
2. Valley District, 4/19/1915
3. Thornton Luttge District, 3/29/1922
4. Sherlock Drive District, 10/16/1922
5. Magnolia Park District, 10/6/1923
6. Moreland District, 3/10/1924
7. Sunset Canyon District, 1/18/1926
8. Benmar Hills Addition, 3/1/1948
9. McClure Addition, 1/21/1954
10. Grandview Highlands, 8/19/1954
11. Keswick Addition, 8/16/1955
12. Horace Mann School Site, 10/19/1955
13. Cabrini Addition, 2/4/1959
14. North Hollywood Addition, 8/22/1967
15. Frederic Street Annexation, 4/10/1979

Annexation Map

The Roaring Twenties, the decade between the end of the Great War and the Depression following the stock market crash, was a period of growth and real estate development that shaped the Burbank community. The population had grown to 2,913. Automobiles were filling city streets, and travelers were coming in and out of town.

The Burbank Police Department was established and patrolled the streets; the volunteer fire department became a three-man paid department under Chief Homer Davis; and the Burbank Chamber of Commerce was established in 1920 to help promote economic growth and prosperity in the city.

In 1919, real estate developer Ben W. Marks planned to subdivide and develop a six thousand-acre ranch he purchased from Oliver J. Stough to create Benmar Hills. This would be the first development on the northwest side of Burbank. Due to its proximity to downtown Burbank, Benmar Hills was integrated into the city and essentially became part of a model-city master plan. The property was located at the foot of the Verdugo Mountains, on the north side of the commercial core along what is now San Fernando Boulevard.

Marks planned to build an industrial park, residential tracts, country club, hotel, and a new civic center. He donated a parcel to the City to build the Burbank Civic Center

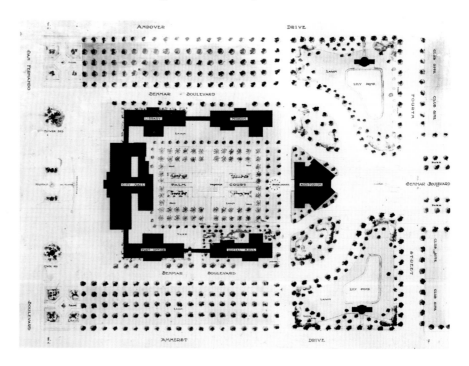

(now McCambridge Park). The Benmar property was also considered a potential site to build the University of California at Los Angeles. Although the five hundred-acre parcel appeared to be a promising contender, Westwood was chosen as the future home for UCLA. As a reminder of Ben Marks's grand vision, university-named streets in the tract—such as Harvard, Dartmouth, and Amherst—still exist.

In 1921, the Sunset Canyon Country Club and nine-hole golf course was completed adjacent to the city's northeastern border. The property covered 1,300 acres and extended along Sunset Canyon Drive from Orange Grove Avenue to Verdugo Avenue and to the top of Country Club Drive. It was followed by a new country club, located on Sunset Canyon Drive and Orange Grove Avenue. Nestled in the Verdugo Mountains, the exclusive country club had a golf course, swimming pool, and was often used as a location for motion pictures. However, years later a fire consumed the Verdugo Mountains, followed by torrential rains and mudslides. The cleanup from this natural disaster caused the country club to go bankrupt, and the City would eventually annex the property in 1926. Today, the Sunset Canyon Country Club building and much of the surrounding property is owned by the Church of Jesus Christ of Latter-Day Saints.

Facing Page: Benmar Hills Development brochure.
Top Right: Original Sunset Canyon Country Club, 1927.
Middle Right: New Sunset Canyon Country Club, 1939.
Bottom: Golfers at the Sunset Canyon Country Club, 1932.
Photos courtesy of Burbank Historical Society.

As real estate continued to develop, so did the need to provide more schools. Burbank High School was built in the new Benmar development and completed in 1922. The original High School was converted into John Muir Junior High School. Abraham Lincoln and Joaquin Miller elementary schools were added the following year.

The Providencia Methodist Church was originally constructed in 1888, torn down in 1919, and replaced in 1922 by a new church, First Methodist Church. This building was located on the corner of Third Street and Olive Avenue and was eventually demolished in 1952 to make way for the Los Angeles County Courthouse.

The Magnolia Park residential development transformed the southwestern part of Burbank. Earl L. White, the owner of a lucrative dairy ranch in the area adjacent to Oak Street and Hollywood Way, converted his dairy land to smaller parcels and created the Magnolia Park subdivision. In 1923, he began to build streets, install public utilities, and lay curbs and sidewalks. When White was not able to obtain City funding to create a shortcut from Burbank to Hollywood via the Cahuenga Pass, he cleared the brush up to Dark Canyon (Barham Boulevard) himself and named the street Hollywood Way.

RECENT DEVELOPMENT
MAGNOLIA PARK
EARL L. WHITE

Top: Aerial view of Burbank and Magnolia boulevards, 1928.

Middle Left: Union High School, 1922.

Middle Right: Magnolia Park Development brochure.

Right: Magnolia Park, circa 1920.

Photos courtesy of Burbank Historical Society.

White built a two-story bank, service station, auto repair garage, dry goods store, and barber and beauty shops at the corner of Magnolia Boulevard and Pioneer Avenue (now known as Hollywood Way). By 1926, construction was completed on the Magnolia Park Methodist Church on Hollywood Way, the city's first radio station (KELW), and the *Burbank Tribune* newspaper. John Burroughs Junior High School was completed the same year, and later the school would become a senior high school in 1948.

In 1927, Burbank formalized its governing system by adopting a city charter. This established Burbank as a general law city, which would be managed by a five-member City Council.

Above: John Burroughs Junior High graduation, 1931. Photo courtesy of Burbank Historical Society.

Inset: Octavia Lesueur helped author the City Charter; was a founding member of St. Jude's Episcopal Church, the Zonta Club for Women, and the Realty Board; served as the first president of the Park and Forestry Commission; and was instrumental in planting 30,000 trees in Burbank.

[Business and Industry]

New business and industry moved to Burbank. The motion picture studios and the aircraft industry soon established roots that would provide financial stability for the growing community.

In 1926, First National Pictures moved to a parcel of land formerly owned by Dr. Burbank and built a studio on the property. After the success of Warner Bros. film *The Jazz Singer*, the world's first talkie, its company's founders—Albert, Sam, Harry, and Jack L. Warner—purchased First National Pictures in 1928, gaining ownership of the newly built studio. The Warners invested heavily into converting the studio into the finest movie production facility in the world.

In 1928, Allan Loughead (later changed name to Lockheed) opened the Lockheed Aircraft Company in Burbank. The manufacturing plant was located in the former Empire China Company and Mission Glass Works buildings near an intersection called "Turkey Crossing" at San Fernando Boulevard and Empire Avenue. The company would build the Lockheed Vega Aircraft, best known for the record-setting solo flight across the Atlantic piloted by Amelia Earhart.

Top: First National Pictures. Photo courtesy of Burbank Historical Society.

Bottom: Lockheed B-1 plant and Southern Pacific Railroad (also known as Turkey Crossing), 1947.

Just as America was on the brink of great strides in industry and technology, the 1929 stock market crash brought economic growth to a grinding halt, and the Great Depression would strain the nation. U.S. President Franklin D. Roosevelt launched several economic recovery and relief programs to combat the social and economic stress of the financial collapse.

Although the Great Depression had an effect on Burbank, City leaders looked optimistically toward the future. Economic recovery programs, such as the Works Progress Administration (WPA), cleared the way for Burbank's expansion as the unemployed were put to work paving streets, building flood-control channels, and cutting firebreaks and roads into the Verdugo foothills. Burbank's early commitment to the aircraft industry and motion picture studios significantly helped the local economy survive.

By 1930, the Burbank population had grown to 16,622. On Memorial Day, United Airport was dedicated and would later become the largest airfield in Los Angeles. In 1931, various civic projects were completed. In order to better reflect Burbank as an urban community, a new City seal was created the same year to replace the cantaloupe.

Top: Lockheed. Photo courtesy of Lockheed Martin.

Middle: United Airport opening, 1930.

In 1932, Robert E. Gross and a group of investors bought the bankrupt Lockheed Aircraft Company. Gross was named chairman of the Lockheed Corporation and devised plans to build the Model-10 Electra passenger airplane, the same aircraft that would be flown by Amelia Earhart during the final monumental challenge to become the first woman to fly around the world. Lockheed would soon manufacture a number of aircraft and pilot them down the dirt runway located between Empire Avenue and the railroad tracks. The Sirius was built for Charles Lindbergh, and a custom P-12 and the C-69, Constellation were built for Howard Hughes, owner of Trans World Airlines.

The expansion of the Lockheed manufacturing plant and airport and the growth of the local motion picture studios and various other industries in the city led to an accelerated need for housing, programs, and services. Magnolia Park development continued with the construction of several single- and multi-family homes. Construction was completed on a new library building located on Olive Avenue, the Burbank City Federal Credit Union was established, and the first live performance of the Burbank Symphony was held at the natural bowl amphitheatre (what later became Starlight Bowl), located in Stough Park.

Business and industry growth was also leading the path to more commercial development in the city. Motion picture companies continued to relocate to Burbank. In 1934, Columbia Pictures Corporation acquired a forty-acre plot located at the corner of Hollywood Way and Oak Street and named the facility the Columbia Ranch.

Following the 1937 success of the animated feature film, *Snow White and the Seven Dwarfs*, Walt Disney was looking to expand production and move to a larger site. In 1939, The Walt Disney Company moved to Burbank, built state-of-the-art studios to produce a series of successful animated features, and released *Pinocchio* and *Fantasia*.

Top Right: Burbank Symphony Orchestra performs at Stough Park. Photo courtesy of Burbank Historical Society.

Middle Right: The Walt Disney Studios. Photo courtesy of Burbank Historical Society.

Bottom: Burbank Library located on Olive Avenue.

[World War II]

In the early 1940s, the population in Burbank doubled to 34,337; Lockheed Aircraft Company purchased the United Airport and renamed it Lockheed Air Terminal; World War II was declared following the attack on Pearl Harbor; and Burbank immediately shifted gears to become a wartime industrial complex. The Army Corps of Engineers took measures to protect the aircraft industry and the airport from enemy bombers. Manufacturing facilities were disguised by an elaborate camouflage system. From the air, Lockheed and Vega Airplane manufacturing plants and the airport appeared to be a peaceful valley with farmhouses, trees, and fields of grain and alfalfa. This was accomplished with false construction on actual buildings, artificial treetops on telephone poles, and airfield runways painted with various colors. The parking lots were disguised as alfalfa fields that were actually acres of chicken wire soaked in glue and covered with chicken feathers.

Top Right: Lockheed camouflage.
Left: Lockheed Airport camouflage.
Photos courtesy of Lockheed Martin.

The City also initiated blackouts, constructed air-raid sirens, and established an air-raid headquarters in the basement of the new, yet unfinished, City Hall. The community was organized into sections, and Civil Defense air wardens were appointed to represent each section. Contingents of soldiers were stationed in the community to man searchlights and anti-aircraft equipment placed at strategic positions throughout the city and surrounding foothills. Victory gardens were planted to supplement the food supply. Thousands of citizens went to work to help manufacture military aircraft. Vega Aircraft claimed credit for developing the iconic slogan, "Rosie the Riveter," as women were employed to perform industrial work of welders and riveters in manufacturing jobs. Lockheed and Vega employed thousands to work daytime and nighttime shifts and produce more than 19,000 planes for the nation's war effort.

The war effort also included construction on a United Service Organization (USO) headquarters, located at Olive Avenue Park (now Izay Park). The building was completed in 1942 using joint funds from the City of Burbank and the federal government and provided recreation facilities and dances for both enlisted personnel and the local community. The U.S. government eventually sold the building, and the City took over operations of what is now Olive Recreation Center. The City also received assistance from the Works Progress Administration (WPA) to complete construction on the new City Hall located on Olive Avenue. The building was dedicated to "freedom and justice" in 1943.

As the war ended, temporary housing facilities were set up in Burbank for returning military personnel and relocated Japanese-Americans. Military service staff and their families were afforded temporary barracks at Glenoaks (McCambridge) Park and Lomita Street and Magnolia Boulevard. Japanese-Americans returning from internment camps were provided temporary housing at Winona Avenue and Hollywood Way.

Middle: Olive Avenue Park sign. Photo courtesy of Burbankia

Bottom: Winona Housing Project.

Although war production decreased, Burbank industry continued to prosper. New businesses—including Hydro-Aire (1943), St. Joseph Hospital (1944), Borrmann Steel Company (1945), Burbank Creamery (1946), and Hydra Electric and Aramark (1948)—moved into town and added to the postwar economy. Once again, City officials approved a new City seal to better reflect the community and the support of the aircraft and media industries.

The Burbank media industry soon made news in 1945 during "Hollywood Black Friday." Confederation of Studio Unions (CSU) workers had been on strike and picketing the studios for six months. Disney and several independent studios had bargained with CSU, but many of the other major studios had not. Later that year, Los Angeles and Glendale police were called to support Burbank police and Warner

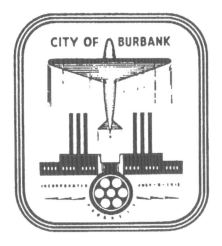

Top Right: Debbie Reynolds at the Verdugo Park Swimming Pool dedication ceremony, 1948.

Middle: Hall-of-Fame baseball pitcher Satchel Paige during spring training in Burbank. Photo courtesy of Luminary Group LLC.

Bottom: St. Louis Browns manager Rogers Hornsby is welcomed to spring training in Burbank, California, by Mayor Walter W. Mansfield (first right) and Al Rediger (second right), president of the Burbank Chamber of Commerce, 1952. Photo courtesy of Burbank Historical Society.

Bros. security when the CSU strike boiled over into a riot in front of Warner Bros. Following national attention, negotiations resumed, and the strike eventually was settled.

Returning military came home to start families and careers and launched the birth of the "Baby Boomer" generation. New housing tracts and recreation facilities were needed. In 1948, Verdugo Park swimming pool and bathhouse were completed. Miss Burbank—Mary Frances "Debbie" Reynolds—was part of the dedication ceremony. Lockheed sponsored the Miss Burbank competition. Reynolds entered the competition on a lark to receive a silk blouse and free lunch. After being crowned Miss Burbank at age sixteen, she signed a motion picture contract with Warner Bros. Studios.

From 1949 to 1952, the City of Burbank entered into a contract with the St. Louis Browns professional baseball team for use of the Olive Avenue Memorial Stadium as a spring training headquarters. The Browns played nine exhibition games, including two against the world-champion Cleveland Indians. An estimated 32,000 spectators attended the Browns routine workouts and games. Burbank was fortunate to see famous Hall-of-Fame pitcher Satchel Paige play for the Browns and Hall-of-Fame baseball player Rogers Hornsby manage the team in 1952.

[The 1950s]

© NBC Universal, Inc.

In the 1950s, Burbank teenagers were wearing poodle skirts and blue jeans, bouffant and crew-cut hairstyles, and listening to the new sounds of rock 'n roll and Elvis Presley. U.S. President Harry Truman authorized military forces to be sent to Korea. An armistice agreement was signed in 1953 and military personnel began returning home.

The Burbank community continued to grow, the population doubled to 78,577, and commercial development expanded. In 1949, Burt Baskin and Irv Robbins bought the Burbank Creamery located on Victory Boulevard. Baskin and Robbins could now supervise production of their own ice cream products, and by 1953 the first Baskin-Robbins 31 Flavors ice cream store opened. Several other new businesses moved into town, including Wells Fargo Bank (1950) and California Kitchens Inc. (1954). In 1955, Robert W. Miller and Maurie and Harry Liff opened five retail stores called United Merchandising Corp. (now Big 5 Sporting Goods).

In 1952, another media mogul moved into Burbank. NBC-TV relocated its television headquarters from Hollywood to a new facility on Olive and Alameda avenues. In 1955, NBC officially opened a new color television studio built specifically for color broadcasts. The dedication ceremonies included the first color telecast from the West Coast titled *Entertainment 1955*, featuring guests Bob Hope, Dinah Shore, Judy Holliday, Ralph Edwards, James Stewart, and Helen Hayes.

In 1952, Warner Bros. Studios was struck by two major backlot fires that destroyed several structures and sets. Dr. David Burbank's ranch house, still standing on the Warner Bros. property at the time of the fire, was completely destroyed.

Top: NBC Burbank Studios. Photo courtesy of NBCU Photo Bank.

Middle: Warner Bros. fire, 1952. Photo courtesy of Burbankia.

Right: NBC groundbreaking. Photo courtesy of Burbank Historical Society.

As the community continued to grow, so did the need for housing and recreational facilities on the northeast side of town. In 1957, a WPA construction project at McCambridge Park (formerly Glenoaks Park) was completed and the community center and swim stadium were opened to the community.

In 1958, philanthropist, humanitarian, and California pioneer Joseph A. DeBell donated one hundred acres of land to the City to build a golf course and clubhouse, provided the facility be built in one year. In 1959, DeBell Municipal Golf Course was officially dedicated. Radio and recording artist "Tennessee" Ernie Ford took part in the first round of golf. The same year, Full O' Life—one of the first modern health food supermarkets and restaurants in the western United States—opened, and it is still located on Magnolia Boulevard. Community Chevrolet also opened a car dealership on Olive Avenue.

"Beautiful Downtown Burbank™"

The 1960s was a period of growth and social change. Military troops were sent to Vietnam, and the Civil Rights Act was passed in 1964 forbidding discrimination based on gender or ethnicity. Burbank Baby Boomers were becoming teenagers whose fashion style included miniskirts and go-go boots.

Just as the nineteenth-century construction of the railroad linked Burbank with the rest of Southern California, the Ventura and Golden State freeways would link Burbank with the rest of the state. In 1961, six miles of the Golden State Freeway through Burbank was completed, linking Northern and Southern California. The next year, the Ventura Freeway opened an east-west passage through Burbank and across the San Fernando Valley.

Top Left: Construction of Golden State Freeway, 1957. Photo courtesy of Burbankia.

Bottom Left: Olive Avenue bridge over the Golden State Freeway opened in 1958.

Right: Golden Mall, 1967. Photo courtesy of Burbank Historical Society.

In 1960, Americans were watching popular television programs like the *Andy Griffith Show* and *My Three Sons*. Some of Burbank's own stepped into the spotlight. Ron Howard was cast to play Opie Taylor on the *Andy Griffith Show*. Howard would be featured on this popular television program for the next eight years. Don Grady was cast in *My Three Sons* to play the eldest son, Robbie. In 1965, Debbie Reynolds became one of the most sought-after female celebrities. After starring in a number of motion pictures, she was nominated for an Academy Award for *The Unsinkable Molly Brown*.

In 1966, a fire started in the kitchen of the Skyroom Restaurant of the Lockheed Air Terminal. The tower and the entire second floor were completely destroyed. Air traffic was safely diverted to nearby Van Nuys Airport and Los Angeles International Airport. Despite the tremendous damage, the airport reopened the next day, and the tower and terminal were rebuilt the following year.

In 1967, the traffic-free, open-air "Golden Mall" was dedicated, changing the face of San Fernando Boulevard by converting several central blocks into the pedestrian shopping district. However, completion of the Burbank Boulevard bridge and Golden State Freeway in the 1960s began to divert traffic away from downtown Burbank and divided the city into two parts. Although the "Golden Mall" was intended to revitalize downtown and increase sales, mall traffic declined over the years, eventually leading to its closure.

In 1968, *Rowan and Martin's Laugh-In* became a regular comedy variety show on NBC. The show starred Dan Rowan and Dick Martin and featured a comedy ensemble including Ruth Buzzi, Judy Carne, Henry Gibson, Goldie Hawn, Larry Hovis, Arte Johnson, and Jo Anne Worley. Memorable

Top Right: Larry L. Maxam attended Burbank High School, enlisted in the U.S. Marine Corps in 1965, and was stationed in Vietnam. Corporal Maxam was posthumously awarded the Medal of Honor by President Richard Nixon for "conspicuous gallantry and intrepidity at the risk of his life above and beyond the call of duty."

Bottom Right: Fire at Lockheed Air Terminal, 1966. Photo courtesy of Lockheed Martin.

characters and catch phrases such as "Sock it to me," "Here comes the judge," and "Verrry interesting" became part of the era's pop culture. The show opened with a skit featuring a campy old-fashioned radio booth announcer played by Gary Owens, who introduced the cast and jokingly referred to NBC's Burbank production facility as "Beautiful Downtown Burbank™." For the next six years, Burbank was featured in a series of sketches that made fun of the community. However, the reality was that Burbank was a city that had grown to a population of 97,262, and "Beautiful Downtown Burbank™" was moving toward becoming the epicenter of the entertainment industry. NBC, The Walt Disney Company, and Warner Bros. were producing television and feature films, and aerospace leader Lockheed employed as many as 80,000 people.

Right: Rowan and Martin's Laugh-In. Pictured: Arte Johnson (front); (l-r, second row) Ruth Buzzi, Dan Rowan, Dick Martin, Goldie Hawn; (third row) Henry Gibson, Judy Carne, Gary Owens, Eileen Brennan, Willie Tyler; (back row) Teresa Graves, Richard Dawson, Jo Anne Worley, Alan Sues.

Left: Ruth Buzzi and Arte Johnson during a *Laugh-In* scene. The original Ruth Buzzi bench was donated to the City and placed at Mc-Cambridge Park.

Bottom: The Tonight Show Starring Johnny Carson. (l-r) Band leader Doc Severinsen, host Johnny Carson, and Ed McMahon.

Photos courtesy of NBCU Photo Bank.

[The 1970s]

Right: Construction of homes above Brace Park, 1970.

Bottom: One of several "castles" built by Bandy Hinge, Inc. in the 1970s and 1980s.

Social changes continued into the 1970s with Vietnam, civil rights, and the energy crisis taking center stage. Bell-bottom jeans, platform shoes, hot pants, and leisure suits were all the fashion rage. Television audiences were watching Garry Marshall's hit comedy, *Happy Days*, starring Burbank's own Ron Howard, Anson Williams, and Erin Moran. NBC's *The Tonight Show Starring Johnny Carson* moved from New York City and began broadcasting from "Beautiful Downtown Burbank™."

The 1970s also marked the beginning of major changes for Burbank. In 1970, the Burbank Redevelopment Agency was formed to enhance the city's economic base through recycling of underutilized and blighted properties. The first Redevelopment Project Area was the Golden State area east of the airport. Throughout the 1970s, former aerospace and other dilapidated industrial buildings were replaced with new buildings and new businesses with aid from the Redevelopment Agency.

The City Centre Redevelopment Project Area was established in the downtown area in 1971. The primary focus became the assembly of a forty-one-acre site for the

Golden Mall shown here under construction became the focus of redevelopment to revitalize the downtown area.

construction of a shopping mall and the revitalization of the ailing Golden Mall. Throughout the late 1970s and early 1980s, the Redevelopment Agency purchased properties and demolished old houses and other rundown buildings.

On February 9, 1971, Burbank was awakened by the 6.6 magnitude Sylmar Earthquake that struck the Los Angeles area. The north San Fernando Valley was hardest hit with sixty-four dead and more than one thousand injured. Burbank reported structural damage, flooding from burst pipes, and some minor fires. Electrical power in Burbank was out and a water reservoir located near Sunset Canyon had to be drained. The Pacific Evangelical United Brethren Home for seniors at Harvard Road and Glenoaks Boulevard suffered major damage. The building was eventually demolished and replaced with the Harvard Plaza high-rise residential buildings that stand on the site today.

In 1977, California voters passed Proposition 13, which amended the State Constitution and reduced property tax rates. Proposition 13 also affected the financial ability of local governments to maintain public services for the community, Burbank being no exception. After initial reductions, tax revenues gradually increased through property owner-

ship changes, user fees, and the construction of new developments. The city was able to expand enterprise funding to cover the cost of certain services, establish user fees, and continue to effectively serve the community.

In 1978, a modern City seal was adopted and is still used today. The seal features City Hall, an airplane to symbolize the aircraft industry, and a strip of film and stage light to represent motion picture production. The bottom portion of the seal depicts the sun rising over the Verdugo Mountains.

Also in 1978, Burbank was one of three cities that created the Burbank-Glendale-Pasadena Airport Authority. The joint powers authority was created to purchase the Hollywood-Burbank Airport from Lockheed. For the first time since its opening in 1930, the airport was owned by a government agency and became known as the Burbank-Glendale-Pasadena Airport. In 1979, Burbank, Glendale, and Pasadena again partnered, this time to create the Verdugo Fire Communications Center, a joint venture among the three cities to provide dispatch services for the three fire departments. The center began operations in 1981 and has become a model for emergency dispatch and communications and today serves twelve cities.

[The 1980s]

Thousands of Burbankers gathered to watch the Olympic Torch pass through Burbank for the 1984 Los Angeles Olympic Games.

The 1980s saw the beginning of the information age and new concepts in entertainment with personal computers, video games, the compact disc, and MTV. The City Council entered the information age in 1987, when the Public Information Office began televising City Council meetings on the public access cable channel. Since then, the Burbank Channel has televised Planning Board, Park, Recreation and Community Services Board, Burbank Unified School District Board meetings, and public affairs programs. In 1984, when Los Angeles hosted the Olympics, Burbank participated in the Olympic Torch Relay and Olympic Flag Project. Verdugo Swimming Pool was chosen as the Olympic training site for the Summer Olympic Games.

Redevelopment of Burbank's downtown area took off in the early 1980s with the construction of the Holiday Inn hotel, office buildings at Glenoaks and Magnolia boulevards, new restaurants along First Street, and other buildings that began to change the face of downtown. A major step toward the revitalization of downtown was the opening of the AMC 10 Theatres on Palm Avenue in 1986. This marked the return of the indoor movie theatre to Burbank since the closing of the Cornell Theatre in the late 1970s. The theatre was joined by Fuddruckers and other restaurants that would be the first of many in the downtown area, including Tony Roma's, Crocodile Cafe, and Great Grill. Downtown's evolution from the Golden Mall was completed in 1990 when San Fernando Boulevard was reopened to traffic where the Golden Mall once stood.

Top: Several high-rise buildings appeared in the Media District during the 1980s.

Bottom: The AMC 10 Theatre started the revitalization of Downtown Burbank when it opened in 1986.

The Media District also saw substantial redevelopment during the 1980s, beginning with the creation of the West Olive Redevelopment Project Area in 1976. Aside from the major studios of Warner Bros., Disney, and NBC, the Media District was home to abandoned and rundown motels, houses, and commercial buildings. Redevelopment efforts in the 1980s led to the revitalization of many properties and the construction of several high-rise buildings, most notably the Disney Channel and Geiger Tower buildings located on Alameda Avenue.

The sudden appearance of several high-rise buildings sparked concern among residents in regard to traffic and the visual quality of the area. This led to the adoption of the Media District Specific Plan in 1991, which placed limitations on the future development of property in the area and ensured that nearby residential neighborhoods would be protected from additional development.

Burbank leaders understood the importance of the media industry to the city's continued prosperity. Burbank had become home to dozens of movies and television shows throughout the 1980s, many of which were filmed at The Burbank Studios, the studio facility operated jointly by Warner Bros. and Columbia Pictures since 1972. In addition to Warner Bros., Columbia had long had a presence in Burbank with its Columbia Ranch property located along Hollywood Way and Oak Street. Columbia Ranch served as a rural backdrop for a number of Columbia Pictures film productions and popular television shows, including *Father Knows Best, Dennis the Menace, Bewitched, I Dream of Jeannie,* and *The Partridge Family*. In the 1970s, Columbia joined forces with Warner Bros. Studios to form The Burbank Studios, and the companies shared ownership of the Ranch.

In 1989, Warner Bros. Studios gained complete ownership of the property and renamed it the Warner Ranch. The property, which is near the main Warner Bros. lot, houses five soundstages and various exterior sets, including Park Boulevard and Blondie Street.

Multi-family residential development exploded in the mid- and late 1980s, with hundreds of new apartment and condominium units being built each year. One of the most notable projects was the Promenade (now Avalon) Apartments built in the downtown area, which became a major feature of the downtown's revitalization. The amount of multi-family development led to a backlash and the adoption of Measure One by voter initiative in 1989. Measure One was a growth-control measure that prohibited the City Council from increasing the residential density limits without voter approval.

The Promenade Apartments, built in 1987, were some of the many residential units built in Burbank during the late 1980s. It was later renovated and renamed Avalon Apartments (inset).

The 1990s

The 1990s brought more big changes for Burbank. After years of assembling property and going through several different developers and proposals throughout the 1980s, the Media City Center mall was finally completed and opened in 1991 with three major department stores and IKEA Home Furnishings store.

The downtown area continued to evolve into the 1990s with the construction of a second tower at the Holiday Inn, and office buildings by family developers Tunnicliffe and Cusumano. The last major manufacturer in the downtown area, the Andrew Jergens Company, closed its plant in 1992 after more than sixty years in Burbank. Senior housing came downtown in 1990 with Tunnicliffe's Golden Palms Apartments, followed by the Wesley and Verdugo Towers projects

Top and Middle Right: The forty-one-acre site sat vacant for several years before a mall project was approved.

Bottom Left and Right: The Media City Center mall opened in 1991 and was later renamed Burbank Town Center.

BURBANK
RECYCLE CENTER
500 SOUTH FLOWER STREET

on Verdugo Avenue and Gangi Development's Silverwinds in 1999. The success of the AMC 10 Theatre spurred its expansion to fourteen screens. The downtown area also saw the development of new civic buildings. The Police and Fire Departments moved into their modern headquarters in 1998.

Regular train service returned to downtown Burbank in 1992 with the birth of the Metrolink commuter rail service. A passenger platform was constructed on the site of the original train depot, which was demolished after suffering major fire damage. In 1998, the Regional Intermodal Transportation Center (later renamed Downtown Burbank Station) was completed on the site, which linked the train platform with bus service, bicycle facilities, and other amenities.

In the 1990s, the Redevelopment Agency's focus on the downtown area expanded south to the South San Fernando Boulevard corridor. The South San Fernando Redevelopment Project Area was established in 1997 to revitalize the corridor that was once U.S. Route 99 and home to numerous car dealers, Menasco Manufacturing, and Moreland Motor Truck Company. Today, the corridor has been substantially revitalized with a streetscape improvement project and recycling of numerous properties with projects such as Ralph's, Trader Joe's, Senior Artists Colony, and San Fernando Walk townhomes.

Meanwhile, other changes were taking place across town

in the Media District. By the 1990s, all three of the major studios were looking to their future needs and requested that the City approve long-term master plans for their properties. The City Council approved master plans for Warner Bros., Disney, and NBC in the 1990s, which cemented the role of the media industry in Burbank. As the major studios prepared for the future, Burbank also saw the end of an era. For thirty years, *The Tonight Show Starring Johnny Carson* was filmed at NBC Studios in Burbank and began with music and the announcement *"Heeeeeere's Johnny!"* Host Johnny Carson also joked about "Beautiful Downtown Burbank™," a catchphrase from *Laugh-In*. In 1992, he retired as late-night talk-show host and entertainer, and comedian Jay Leno would assume the helm. One year later, the Tonight Show

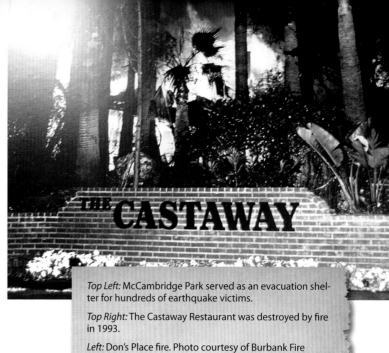

Top Left: McCambridge Park served as an evacuation shelter for hundreds of earthquake victims.

Top Right: The Castaway Restaurant was destroyed by fire in 1993.

Left: Don's Place fire. Photo courtesy of Burbank Fire Department.

Playground was dedicated in Johnny Carson Park through a generous donation by Jay Leno.

Burbank's commitment to become more environmentally conscious and reduce its impact on future generations was solidified. In 1982, the Burbank Recycle Center opened and curbside recycling collection began. In 1992, Burbank launched a nationally acclaimed recycling program as the Burbank Recycle Center moved to a new location on South Flower Street and was able to process five thousand tons of recyclables per month. Soon thereafter, the City implemented automated refuse collection with separate collection for trash, recyclables, and green waste. The City's recycled water system began operation in 1993.

Burbank also suffered losses and near losses in the 1990s. The Castaway Restaurant, known as "the Jewel on the Hill" had been a landmark in Burbank since the 1960s. Located on Harvard Drive in the Verdugo Mountains, above DeBell Golf Course, the Castaway featured breathtaking views of Burbank and the San Fernando Valley and was host to a number of celebrities, weddings, and big events. However, in 1993, the restaurant was nearly lost to fire. Firefighters from Burbank, Glendale, and Pasadena responded to the blaze. It

took approximately three hours to extinguish. Although the fire gutted the kitchen, bar, and dining room, the restaurant reopened the following year.

On January 17, 1994, the 6.7 magnitude Northridge Earthquake struck; the epicenter was approximately ten miles west of Burbank. The Northridge and Santa Clarita Valley areas sustained the most damage from this quake. The American Red Cross opened an evacuation shelter at McCambridge Park to serve hundreds of earthquake victims. The estimated damage to Burbank's public facilities was over $3 million, while the estimate for private facilities was $58 million. Most of the damage was in the Magnolia Park section of the city, primarily around Hollywood Way and Magnolia Boulevard. To help facilitate recovery, the Burbank City Council made $200,000 in community development block grant funds available as no-interest loans for businesses and grants to residents made homeless by the disaster.

Later that year, Burbank bid farewell to the popular "Don's Place" restaurant on Olive Avenue. Following an early morning fire, the local burger joint was reduced to charred remains. Located across from Izay Park for forty years, Don's Place was a popular watering hole for the Los Angeles Rams football team and local residents.

[Twenty-First Century]

As Burbank entered the twenty-first century, the face of the city continued to evolve. The Golden State Project Area started to change dramatically with Lockheed's announcement in 1990 that it was closing all of its Burbank operations. This opened up hundreds of acres for potential redevelopment, as Lockheed's once-busy factories were closed and demolished. After several years of negotiations and environmental cleanup, the B-1 site on Empire Avenue and Victory Place was developed by the Zelman Company into the Burbank Empire Center, a major shopping center complete with Costco, Target, Lowe's, and other major stores.

Meanwhile, the A-1 North property was developed into an airport parking lot and restaurants, while the A-1 South (and former Unimart) property on Hollywood Way became Fry's Electronics. The B-6 property on Hollywood Way was acquired by the Airport Authority and was intended as the site for a new passenger terminal. After years of legal battles with the City, the site remains vacant and its future is unclear. M. David Paul & Associates purchased property along Empire Avenue and began the development of Media Studios North in 1996. Today, the office campus includes multiple office buildings and is home to Yahoo!, Kaiser Permanente, Insomniac Games, and other high-profile companies.

AMC moved across Palm Avenue to the new AMC 16 Theatres in 2003. Today, the downtown area has emerged as a premiere shopping, dining, and entertainment destination. The AMC 16 Theatre is consistently among the top AMC

The Burbank Empire Center opened in 2001 on the former site of a Lockheed aircraft factory.

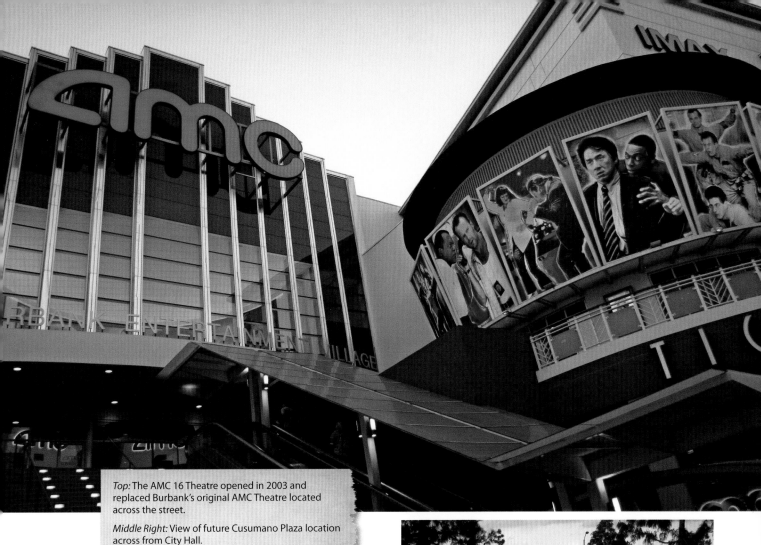

Top: The AMC 16 Theatre opened in 2003 and replaced Burbank's original AMC Theatre located across the street.

Middle Right: View of future Cusumano Plaza location across from City Hall.

Bottom Right: Cusumano Plaza.

theatres nationwide for attendance, while new restaurants and shops continue to come downtown. Additional housing came downtown to create a twenty-four-hour environment with the Village Walk project in 2005 and The Collection project (on the site of the original AMC theatre) in 2008.

The 2000s saw further changes to City offices and facilities. The site of the original City Hall and later the Police Services building across from City Hall was redeveloped into an office building by the Cusumano family, marking the first time since at least 1916 that the property was not used as a government building. The Municipal Services building behind City Hall was demolished in 2001 after suffering damage in the 1994 Northridge Earthquake. Several City departments were relocated into existing buildings across from City Hall and portable trailers until the new Community Services building opened in 2008.

With the continuing expansion of the industry, Burbank became the home of hundreds of media and related support

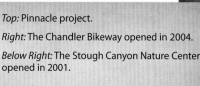

Top: Pinnacle project.

Right: The Chandler Bikeway opened in 2004.

Below Right: The Stough Canyon Nature Center opened in 2001.

companies such as post production, film processing, special effects, equipment rental, and related businesses. The Media District continued to evolve as the M. David Paul Company completed the first phase of the Pinnacle project in 2002, followed soon after by the second phase. Today, the complex houses NBC, Warner Music, and Arnie Morton's Restaurant. Although NBC has announced its intent to depart Burbank, its studio campus will remain a hub for the media industry. M. David Paul purchased the studio property and began building out the master plan, starting with the completion of the Pointe high-rise office tower in 2009. In addition to Warner Bros. and Disney, Burbank today is home to Cartoon Network, Nickelodeon Animation, Yahoo!, Clear Channel, and hundreds of other media companies.

To further demonstrate the City's dedication to providing a high quality of life for its residents, projects such as the Chandler Bikeway, Stough Canyon Nature Center, Robert R. Ovrom Park, and a new and expanded state-of-the-art Buena Vista Branch Library were completed in the early 2000s. The attractive state-of-the-art library facility has become a focal point for the community's informational, educational, and entertainment needs.

In 2000, a Southwest Airlines Boeing 737 overshot the normal landing area and crashed through the blast fence at

Top Right: The new Buena Vista Branch Library opened in 2002.

Middle Right: The Robert R. Ovrom Park and Community Center opened in 2009.

Bottom: The late Mary Alice O'Connor (center), wife of Disney Legend and animator Ken O'Connor, is pictured dedicating Burbank's Mary Alice O'Connor Family Center in 2007 with Cinderella (left) and Fritz Coleman (right). Mary served as the inspiration for the Fairy Godmother in *Cinderella* and filled a similar role for the lives she touched in her many years of service to the community.

Disney character © Disney.

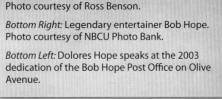

the end of Runway 26, stopping on Hollywood Way. The 137 passengers and flight crew were safely evacuated and six people were transported to local hospitals. Hollywood Way was closed until the next morning. The aircraft was said to have cost $40 million.

In 2003, legendary entertainer Bob Hope passed away. For decades, Hope had entertained troops at military bases, bringing laughter and a bit of home to U.S. servicemen and women overseas. He was also committed to serving the community. He donated land and thousands of dollars for community projects, was a driving force behind the "Defenders

© NBC Universal, Inc.

Golden State Safety Barbeque at Lundigan Park.

of the Constitution" monument located on Riverside Drive, and performed live at the Burbank Starlight Bowl. Hope received many honors and much recognition while he lived in nearby Toluca Lake. A portion of Catalina Street near NBC Studios was renamed Bob Hope Drive in his honor. In 1993, NBC named its studios for the entertainer. Upon his death, a memorial plaque was dedicated in his honor at McCambridge Park War Memorial. The Burbank-Glendale-Pasadena Airport was renamed Bob Hope Airport in 2003 to honor the legendary entertainer. The Olive Avenue Post Office was renamed in 2003 to commemorate both the centennial anniversary of Bob Hope's birth and the Wright Brothers' first flight.

At the turn of the century, the City of Burbank and the Community Development Department began to take a new approach to neighborhood revitalization. In 1997, the department's Redevelopment Agency purchased and rehabilitated nine multi-family rental buildings located in the cul-de-sac of West Elmwood Street. The Elmwood neighborhood was one of the city's most problematic areas and was a prime example of an underserved pocket of the community. Gang activity and physical deterioration created a dangerous blighted environment that generated a noticeable imbalance in quality-of-life standards in comparison to the rest of the city.

In order to centralize agency strategies, the Community Development Department termed Elmwood and other distressed areas in Burbank as "focus neighborhoods." The department incrementally identified four additional focus neighborhoods throughout the city: Verdugo-Lake, Golden State, Peyton-Grismer, and Lake-Alameda. These are designated as target project areas as a result of higher densities and rental unit numbers, deferred maintenance and dilapidation, lower income levels, higher gang activity, higher crime rates, and limited resident access to key services such as parks, open space, and valuable community programs.

The City partnered with the Burbank Housing Corporation (BHC), a private nonprofit housing developer established in 1997, to administer the operation of the neighborhoods' affordable housing units and to help build safe and strong communities with families. Soon housing programs and activity centers were established in the focus neighborhoods. Burbank supported fund-raising efforts for the BHC Al Cottriel Scholarship to be awarded to accomplished focus neighborhood scholars on their way to college. As a result of these improvements and programs, residents have established ties with the community, remained in their households for stable durations, and more and more participating youth became college bound. This is a key measure of success and a positive indicator that building healthy communities is a long-term investment in the future.

Burbank City Hall, circa 1940. Photo courtesy of Burbank Historical Society.

[Chapter Two]

City
Government

Burbank Water and Power | *Established 1913*

Burbank Water and Power (BWP) provides water and electric services to Burbank. The Water Division is responsible for the planning, engineering, construction, operation, and maintenance of the City's potable and recycled water facilities. The Power Supply Division develops, operates, and builds facilities for the generation and delivery of electricity. The Electric Services Division is responsible for the planning, construction, operation, and maintenance of electric stations, power lines, service drops, and meters. This division also maintains the City's street-lighting system, maintains the City's internal radio and telephone equipment, and installs fiber-optic lines.

BWP Olive Power Plant.

Boards and Commissions Supported

▌ Burbank Water and Power Board

Notable Dates and Events in Department History

1912 Bonds are sold for the establishment of a municipal water works; Burbank purchases one water well and a small water system operated by L.C. Brand's El Miradero Water Company.

1913 The first electricity is distributed in Burbank by the newly established Public Service Department; power is supplied by Southern California Edison, and electric lines are purchased from the privately owned Burbank Light and Power Company.

1914 A domestic water works system is established.

1928 Burbank becomes one of thirteen founding members of the Metropolitan Water District (MWD).

1937 The first electricity from Hoover Dam is supplied to Burbank; it remains the city's sole source of electricity until 1941.

1949 The Public Service Department Administration Building is completed.

1967 Burbank power generating plants begin using recycled water for cooling.

1977 The Public Service Department Advisory Board is established to advise the City Council on issues related to the utility.

1986 The first fiber-optic cable is installed in Burbank.

Local groundwater production ends due to the discovery of volatile organic compounds in wells.

1992 The Supervisory Control and Data Acquisition (SCADA) system is completed.

The Granular Activated Carbon Treatment Plant is completed to treat contaminated groundwater.

1993 The Recycled Water System begins operation.

1996 The Burbank Operable Unit is put into service to remove volatile organic compounds from groundwater, allowing local groundwater production to resume.

The citywide fiber-optic cable system begins operation.

2000 The Public Service Department is renamed Burbank Water and Power.

2001 The first commercial landfill power plant using microturbine technology begins operation at the Burbank Landfill.

2005 The Magnolia Power Plant, a 310-megawatt combined cycle plant, is placed into service to provide power to Burbank and five partner communities.

2007 Burbank is the first utility to adopt a 33 percent or higher renewable power portfolio standard.

2010 Optical Network Enterprise Burbank (ONE Burbank) begins operation.

BWP power plant, circa 1940.

City Attorney's Office | *Established 1911*

The City Attorney's Office serves as general counsel to the City Council, Burbank Redevelopment Agency, Housing Authority, Parking Authority, and Youth Endowment Services (YES) Fund Board and is required to attend all meetings. The office provides legal support to City departments for all transactional matters, including agreements, preparation of resolutions and ordinances, legal opinions, and assistance and legal representation to the City Council, all City departments, and the City's boards, commissions, and committees. The City Attorney's Office prosecutes misdemeanor violations of state and local laws; initiates criminal and civil code compliance actions; and represents the city, its officers, and employees in legal actions.

Burbank Courthouse, located at Third Street and Olive Avenue.

Notable Dates and Events in Department History

1911 The City Attorney's Office is established.

1942 The City Attorney becomes a full-time position.

1992 Burbank becomes the first city in California to successfully obtain a restraining order against local street-gang members; the civil injunction becomes a successful model throughout the state.

1999 The Victim Restitution Program is established, which is unique to Burbank.

City Clerk's Office | *Established 1911*

The City Clerk's Office is the official keeper of City records. The City Council, other City departments, and the public rely on the City Clerk's Office to provide information regarding the operations and legislative history of the City. The City Clerk's Office is charged with conducting elections and maintaining all official records and serves as the filing officer for campaign statements and Statements of Economic Interest required by law. The office publishes all ordinances adopted by the City Council; advertises notices of public hearings, bid openings, and other legal notices; administers the Records Management Program; and maintains a comprehensive annual historical collection.

City Clerk, Emily Peyton Forbes, 1916.

City Clerk's Office, 1917.

Notable Dates and Events in Department History

1911 City Clerk's Office is established.

1927 City Clerk position is changed from appointed to elected.

1951 Election results are projected on a curtain in the City Council Chamber, which for the first time allowed the public and the press to follow election results as they were tabulated.

1954 First photocopying machine is installed in the City Clerk's office to make copies of City Council agenda packets.

1957-58 First Burbank Election Code is prepared.

1963 Pilot program starts to microfilm permanent City records.

1965 Office produces first edition of *A Thumbnail Sketch* publication, which has been updated annually every year since.

1972-73 City Records Center is established and Centralized Records Management System implemented.

2000 Electronic Document Imaging/Management System (EDMS) is established.

2001 First election is held entirely by mail (Restore Our Airport Rights/Measure A special election).

2005 Burbank becomes first city in California to conduct regular municipal elections exclusively by mail-in ballot.

2007 Granicus online system is implemented to provide online integrated access to agendas and staff reports along with live broadcasting of City Council meetings.

City Council Office | *Established 1911*

The City Council enacts the laws and establishes administrative policy for the City government. In order to serve the City as a council member, a citizen must be elected by the voters of the City. The individual must be a citizen of the United States, must be a qualified elector of the City of Burbank, and must have resided in Burbank for at least one month.

Council meetings are usually held once a week, during which the Council is presented with reports and recommendations from staff. The Council makes motions, adopts resolutions and ordinances, and generally directs financial and operational policy.

The mayor is chosen by the Council for a one-year term to preside over meetings and represent the City Council at events and functions. The mayor has the same voting power as any other member of the Council.

City Council, 2010: (front) Mayor Anja Reinke, (back L-R) Vice Mayor Jess Talamantes, Dr. David Gordon, Gary Bric, and Dave Golonski.

Above: City Council Chambers, circa 1980.

Below: Councilman looking at foam in the City Hall fountain.

Notable Dates and Events in Department History

1911 The Board of Trustees is established with the incorporation of Burbank; the head of the Board is known as the president of the Board of Trustees.

1927 The Board of Trustees is changed to the City Council, and the president of the Board of Trustees is changed to the mayor, with the adoption of the City Charter.

1943 A public address system is installed in the City Council chambers.

1971 Smoking is banned in City Council meetings.

1987 City Council meetings are broadcast to residents via the local access cable television channel; Burbank becomes one of only fifty cities in California to televise meetings at that time.

2001 The City Council chambers and mural restoration are completed; except for modern conveniences, the chambers and the murals are restored to their 1943 appearance, reversing alterations made in 1964 and 1978.

2002 The California Supreme Court declines to review a decision by the 2nd District Court of Appeals, ruling that only non-sectarian prayer is permitted during City Council meetings.

2007 City Council meetings are broadcast and archived via the Internet.

2008 Because of potential threats, metal detectors are used for the first time at the entrance to the City Council chambers for the safety of visitors and employees.

2010 A random phone survey conducted of Burbank residents reveals a 94 percent satisfaction with City services and a 96 percent satisfaction with overall quality of life in Burbank.

City Manager's Office | *Established 1927*

The City launched its new website in 2009.

Bomb shelter under construction across from City Hall, 1960.

Notable Dates and Events in Department History

1927 The city manager position is created by the City Charter.

1965 City Manager Harmon Bennett is quoted saying, "Burbank has many of the assets of a small town without the usual insularity of a small town and the leanings toward barren provincialism."

1968 The first community newsletter is issued, called "Burbank Progress"; 35,000 copies are distributed quarterly to all Burbank households.

1970 Employee communications are improved through the new employee *Hotline* newsletter, which is distributed with each paycheck.

The first town hall meetings are held to improve communication with the public.

1971 A new Information Center is created to assist visitors to City Hall; a twenty-four-hour phone line is also implemented for reporting complaints.

1995 The City launches its first website; it is upgraded with a new look in 2001 and completely revamped and improved in 2009.

2010 Communications with employees, residents, and businesses are improved through a new electronic newsletter and new monthly newsletter mailed with each utility bill.

The city manager is appointed by the City Council to be the chief executive, administrative, and financial officer of the City government. The city manager, in turn, appoints all officers and employees of the City except elected officials and other appointees of the Council. The city manager and assistant city manager or deputy city managers advise the council on the future needs of the community and recommend actions. Ultimately, the City Manager's Office carries out the policy direction of the Council and is responsible for enforcing all laws and ordinances. Administrative authority is delegated to the various department heads who, in turn, are held accountable by the city manager for rendering the public services assigned to their respective departments. This overall management function is based upon a continuous process of long-range planning, which involves forecasting the City's needs several years in advance, and developing plans for maintaining services given sufficient revenues to meet those demands.

The city manager also oversees the Public Information Office which creates and implements a comprehensive communications program by utilizing various forms of media, including a revamped website that was launched in 2009.

City Council meeting broadcast, 1951.

City Treasurer's Office | *Established 1911*

The City Treasurer's Office is responsible for receiving, disbursing, depositing, and investing all public funds for the City, the Redevelopment Agency, the Youth Endowment Services (YES) Fund, the Parking Authority, and the Housing Authority. The primary objective of the City Treasurer's Office is the safekeeping of City funds.

Burbank State Bank, R. A. Church.

First National Bank, 1916.

Notable Dates and Events in Department History

1911   The first City Treasurer is appointed upon City incorporation (then elected in 1912).

1913   The first bond is passed in Burbank to purchase water and electric distribution systems.

1920s   The first assessments against properties in Burbank are initiated for paving streets and installing streetlights.

1937   A bond is passed for $350,000 to supplement $650,000 in City funds to build a steam-generating plant.

1950s   Walter Hinton becomes the first city treasurer to invest the City's money in interest-bearing accounts.

1994   The Treasurer's Oversight and Review Committee is established.

Financial Services
Department | *Established 1959*

The Financial Services Department maintains the City budget and reports the City's financial condition and the results of its operations in the fiscal year-end Comprehensive Annual Financial Report. The department provides a wide range of services including budget, purchasing, accounts receivable and revenue collection, fixed asset management, payroll, accounts payable, accounting, deferred compensation administration, Public Employees' Retirement System reporting, debt management, and internal audit management.

Notable Dates and Events in Department History

1953 The forerunner of the Financial Services Department is established as the Accounting Bureau within the City Manager's Office; a finance officer position is established to oversee all City financial functions except Water and Power.

1957 The first photocopy machine is purchased, which allows for the first issuing of finance report.

1959 All financial functions including Water and Power, are consolidated under the finance director and new Finance Department.

1971 Various improvements are implemented in department policy and procedure including establishment of a uniform warehouse stock numbering system, creation of an internal audit program, publication of a Standard Office Supplies Catalog, and completion of a Payroll Manual.

1978 California voters approve Proposition 13, creating budget difficulties as property tax revenue decreases.

1984 The Financial Services Department wins its first Certificate of Achievement for Excellence in Financial Reporting from the Government Finance Officers Association, which it has been awarded every year since.

Community Development Department | *Established 1946*

The Community Development Department manages the development of the City; enforces zoning, building, and other City codes; manages housing programs; issues business licenses; and collects business taxes. The department also manages the City's transportation services including BurbankBus, Got Wheels! youth transit, and Senior and Disabled Transportation. The Burbank Redevelopment Agency is part of the department and promotes economic development and redevelopment in the designated redevelopment project areas. The department performs these functions through the Planning and Transportation Division, Building Division, License and Code Services Division, and Housing and Redevelopment Division.

Notable Dates and Events in Department History

1923 The Advisory City Planning Committee to the Board of Trustees is established.

The first Zoning Ordinance is adopted; Burbank is divided into five planning zones: industrial, business, second residential, first residential, and urban/all other.

1924 The first Building Ordinance is adopted.

1925 The City Planning Commission is established.

1942 The Transportation Commission is established.

1945 The first City Master Plan is adopted.

1946 The forerunner of Community Development Department is established as city planning and transportation functions are combined under the Engineer of Planning and Transportation.

The License Bureau is established.

1954 The Planning Commission is changed to the Planning Board.

1965 The first comprehensive General Plan is adopted.

1970 The Burbank Redevelopment Agency is established.

1972 The first Business Tax Ordinance is adopted.

1975 The Burbank Housing Authority is established to operate the Section 8 Rental Assistance Program.

1976 The first Bicycle Master Plan is adopted.

The Residential Rehabilitation Program is established.

1985 The department is reorganized and officially designated as the Community Development Department.

The Landlord Tenant Commission is established.

1994 Burbank Local Transit (BLT) commuter bus service is established to provide transportation between the Downtown Burbank train station and the Media District in conjunction with the new Metrolink commuter rail service.

The Historic Preservation Ordinance is adopted and the Heritage Commission established.

1997 The Burbank Housing Corporation is established to partner with the Redevelopment Agency in providing affordable housing.

2004 The Chandler Bikeway opens.

The first green building standards are adopted.

2005 Burbank Local Transit is renamed BurbankBus and expands routes to other areas of the city.

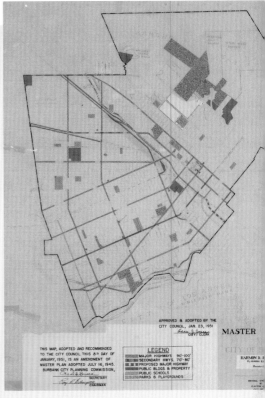

1945 Master Plan.

Boards and Commissions Supported

▌ Board of Building and Fire Code Appeals

▌ Burbank Housing Corporation Board of Directors

▌ Community Development Goals Committee

▌ Heritage Commission

▌ Landlord Tenant Commission

▌ Planning Board

▌ Transportation Commission

Fire Department | *Established 1927*

Home inspection program kickoff, 1957.

T he Fire Department protects the community by preventing and mitigating threats to people, property, and the environment through fire prevention, public education, and emergency response. The department's services include fire suppression, emergency medical response, rescue, hazardous materials response, and disaster preparedness.

Drill Tower, 1955.

Paramedics, circa 1970.

Apparatus and staff outside Station 1, 1950.

Notable Dates and Events in Department History

1909 A volunteer fire department is organized.

1913 The Board of Trustees votes for the City to take control of the volunteer fire department.

1916 The City begins paying volunteer firefighters for each fire response.

The first fire pumper is purchased using bond proceeds.

A new City Hall building is completed at the corner of Olive Avenue and Third Street with a Fire Department annex facing Third Street.

The first fire hydrants are installed in Burbank.

1927 The volunteer fire department is converted from a partly paid, mostly volunteer department to a fully paid Fire Department.

1938 The first Fire Prevention and Regulation Code is adopted.

1944 Burbank Firefighters Local 778 union is established.

1945 The Fire Prevention Bureau is established; fire prevention education in the schools begins with an emphasis on Fire Prevention Week.

1954 The first recruit training class is conducted.

1957 The new Fire Headquarters (Station No. 1) is completed on Olive Avenue.

A fire alarm box system is installed throughout the city with 140 standard alarm boxes and 27 master boxes.

1960 Burbank voters vote to ban the sale and use of all fireworks in Burbank.

1968 The brush clearance ordinance is adopted to require adequate clearance of vegetation around homes in the hillside area.

1972 The fire alarm box system is replaced with a modern radio alarm box system with 207 alarm boxes installed citywide; fire and police radio communications are centralized in a single communications center at Police Headquarters.

1975 Firefighters trained as paramedics begin providing Emergency Medical Services.

1981 The Verdugo Communications Center begins operation under an agreement among Burbank, Glendale, and Pasadena to operate a joint fire communications center.

1989 The hazardous materials program is implemented with the purchase of a hazmat vehicle and training of hazmat personnel.

1998 The new Police/Fire Headquarters building opens.

Harvard fire, September 2005. Photo courtesy of Ross Benson.

Fire engineer testing.

Burbank has faced many challenges over the past one hundred years, including natural and man-made emergencies that have made Burbank proud of its emergency responders and have resulted in some City employees making the ultimate sacrifice and giving their lives in service to the Burbank community.

Burbank has been affected by numerous natural disasters that have impacted other communities, namely earthquakes and floods. Burbank was fortunate to escape major widespread damage in the Long Beach Earthquake of 1933, Sylmar Earthquake of 1971, Whittier Earthquake of 1987, and Northridge Earthquake of 1994, although some of the quakes resulted in serious damage to individual buildings, gas leaks, and chemical spills. Burbank has seen more serious damage, injuries, and fatalities from floods and mudslides, some of which followed brush fires in the Verdugo Mountains. Burbank experienced major floods in 1927, 1933, 1938, 1941, and 1962, some of which caused major damage to buildings and city infrastructure, and resulted in serious injuries and deaths.

Burbank has also seen its share of man-made emergencies—from fires, to plane crashes, to murders and other crimes, and tragedies. The following table is by no means a complete list, but it highlights some of the notable emergencies and tragedies that Burbank has faced and overcome in the past one hundred years.

1914	City Marshal Luther Colson is shot and killed while patrolling along the railroad tracks near Victory Place and Lake Street.
1920	Deputy City Marshal Robert L. Normand is shot and killed after responding to a call to check on three men in a vehicle with the lights out. The men opened fire as Normand approached the car.
1927	Police raid and close down a 1,500-gallon-per-day still, the largest uncovered in the San Fernando Valley up to that time.
	A major brush fire in the Verdugo Mountains burns 7,000 acres (1,410 in Burbank) and destroys 100 homes in Sunset Canyon.
1934	A fire at Warner Bros. First National Studios consumes 11 acres of studio backlot resulting in the death of the studio fire chief, serious injuries to five firefighters, and minor injuries to 41 firefighters.
1945	Clashes between police and striking members of the Conference of Studio Unions outside Warner Bros. Studios turns violent on October 5, which became known as "Black Friday." The violence continues for several days with up to 1,000 picketers confronting 300 police officers from Burbank and other law enforcement agencies. More than 300 picketers are arrested.
1952	Police Chief Elmer Adams resigns along with City Manager Howard Stites and City Council Member Walter Mansfield amid allegations of connections to organized crime and an investigation by the California Commission on Organized Crime.
	Two fires occur at the Warner Bros. Studios in May and July. The July fire consumes 23 acres of buildings and sets and destroys the original ranch house of Dr. David Burbank, located on the Warner Bros. lot.
1953	Burbank resident Mabel Monahan is brutally murdered in her Parkside Avenue home by Barbara Graham and several accomplices during an attempted robbery; Graham and two accomplices would later receive the death penalty for the crime and Graham would be portrayed in a movie.
1957	Two firefighters are injured, one critically, when Truck 1 is struck by a Southern Pacific freight train where Olive Avenue crossed the tracks while responding to an emergency call.
1961	Fire Engineer John Saltisik and two civilians are killed and Firefighter Herman Pitsch is critically injured when Service Rescue 4 is involved in a traffic collision while responding to a fire.
	Police Officers Richard E. Kunkle and Joseph R. Wilson are killed in separate traffic collisions while on their motorcycles.
1964	A brush fire started in Glendale is pushed by driving winds into Burbank. The fire burns

Flooding in Burbank, 1938.

Mudslide in Burbank, 1962.

Fire at Warner Bros., 1952.

across the Burbank hillside all the way to Cabrini Canyon before being stopped. The fire causes minor damage to a few homes but fortunately no homes in Burbank are lost.

1966   The control tower and the Skyroom Restaurant at Lockheed Air Terminal are destroyed by a fire.

1967   Four buildings of the Burbank Aircraft Supply Company, formerly the home of the Moreland truck factory, are destroyed by a major fire.

A fire at the Booth Stables kills two stable hands and 17 horses. The fire is the impetus for a new law requiring fire sprinklers in all commercial stables.

1970   Two major fires occur at the Columbia Ranch (now Warner Bros. Ranch) in January and August.

1974   A major fire at the Columbia Ranch results in the destruction of about 25 percent of the sets at the Ranch including three soundstages. The Chamber of Commerce is holding a Community Fair at the Ranch on the weekend of the fire, and most of the vendor booths are also destroyed.

1980   The Verdugo Brush Fire in November 1980 starts in the La Tuna Canyon area of Los Angeles and quickly spreads into Burbank. Fortunately, no homes are lost although some receive minor damage. About 7,000 acres are burned and City Reservoir No. 1 sustains major damage.

Public Works employees Bruce Burton and David George die at the Water Reclamation Plant due to asphyxiation from toxic hydrogen sulfide gas.

1987   A fast-moving brush fire burns more than 100 acres in the Elmwood Canyon area but does not damage any homes.

1993   The Castaway Restaurant is destroyed by a major fire of suspicious origin.

2000   A Southwest Airlines Boeing 737 overshoots the runway at the Bob Hope Airport and comes to rest on Hollywood Way. Six people are transported to local hospitals with minor injuries. Fortunately there are no major injuries or fatalities.

2003   A Metrolink commuter train collides with a truck at the Buena Vista crossing, derailing the train. The driver of the truck is killed and a train passenger later dies as a result of her injuries.

Police Officer Matthew Pavelka is killed and Officer Greg Campbell is critically wounded during a gunfight that erupts during a drug investigation.

2005   The Harvard Brush Fire starts near the Luau Grounds of the Castaway Restaurant and burns 1,054 acres over several days. Country Club Drive is evacuated at one point, but no homes are lost.

2008   Public Works employee Joseph Cordero dies after being critically injured in an accident while working on a sewer line at the Water Reclamation Plant.

Information Technology
Department | *Established 1970*

The Information Technology Department provides and maintains the City's information technology infrastructure and systems. The department provides planning, design, and programming to enhance existing information systems and development, procurement, and implementation of new systems to meet the City's short- and long-term technology needs.

Public Service Department computer, 1952.

Notable Dates and Events in Department History

1951   The Public Service Department (now Burbank Water and Power) installs punch card–tabulating equipment to facilitate utility billing.

1961   Tabulating equipment is implemented citywide for cost accounting and inventory control.

1966   Tabulating equipment is upgraded to an IBM 1440 disc computer, the City's first modern computer.

1970   The Information Systems Department is established.

1974   The Citizens Data Processing Committee is formed to make recommendations for a new computer system.

1976   An IBM 370-125 mainframe computer system is purchased and installed with applications including utility billing, budget accounting, and the Police Incident System.

1982   An IBM 4341 mainframe computer system is purchased and installed with cost accounting, payroll, and fleet management inventory systems.

2001   Information Systems is separated from Management Services, and the Information Technology Department is established.

Management Services
Department | *Established 1946*

The Management Services Department provides support services involving a wide range of internal administrative functions to City departments including human resources, liability, labor relations, workers' compensation, and safety.

The City of Burbank's WorkForce Connection is a great community asset. The public can utilize a variety of free supportive resources: computers with Internet access, telephones, copiers, and fax machines. This job resource and business assistance center is dedicated to providing high-quality employment-related services to the community.

Work Force Connection is a job resource and business assistance center.

Fourteen- and fifteen-year-old students participating in the city's Summer Trails Program.

Youth participate in a Finance Park workshop as part of the BEST Program—an award-winning on-the-job training program for ages sixteen to twenty-one.

Notable Dates and Events in Department History

1930 The Personnel Board is established.

1939 The Civil Service Board is created by initiative ordinance.

1940 A merit system of employment and promotion is implemented.

1946 The personnel director is appointed as head of the new Civil Service Department.

1966 The Civil Service Department becomes the Personnel Department.

1970 Burbank begins administering its own recruitment and testing for City employees, which had previously been done by Los Angeles County.

1978 The Personnel Department becomes the Administrative Services Department.

1988 The Administrative Services Department becomes the Management Services Department.

Boards and Commissions Supported

❚ Civil Service Board

Library Services Department | *Established 1938*

West Burbank Branch Library, 1954.

The Library Services Department provides the community with access to a variety of services and information resources. The Central Library and two branches offer an extensive collection of print material and other media, Internet access, research staff, and supportive services. The library also provides a variety of youth and adult literacy programs.

Buena Vista Branch Library.

Central Library, circa 1950.

Notable Dates and Events in Department History

1913 The Burbank Public Library is established as a contract branch of the Los Angeles County Library and is located in the Thompson Block Building at San Fernando Boulevard and Olive Avenue.

1935 The first dedicated library building is built at 425 E. Olive Avenue (now the open landscaped area next to the Central Library at the corner of Olive and Glenoaks).

1938 The Burbank Public Library is established as a City department and is separated from the Los Angeles County Library.

1948 The Buena Vista Branch Library opens.

1953 The library begins offering audiovisual materials in the form of records and 16 mm films.

1954 The West Burbank Branch Library opens in a leased storefront on Burbank Boulevard.

1956 The North Glenoaks Branch Library opens in a leased storefront on Irving Drive between Glenoaks Boulevard and Scott Road.

1960 Burbank's Sister City program is established with Solna, Sweden, as the first Sister City; later Burbank gained three more Sister Cities: Gabarone, Botswana; Inchon, Korea; and Ota, Japan.

1963 The new two-story Central Library building opens.

1972 The Northwest Branch Library opens on Victory Boulevard; the West Burbank Branch on Burbank Boulevard is closed.

1978 The North Glenoaks Branch Library closes following passage of Proposition 13.

1980 Friends of the Burbank Public Library, a volunteer non-profit organization that raises funds to support the library, is established.

1992 The Adult Literacy Program is established.

2000 The library begins offering free Internet access to the public.

2002 The new Buena Vista Branch Library building opens.

Central Library, Children's Room, circa 1970.

Ota, Japan, Sister City.

Boards and Commissions Supported

▌ Board of Library Trustees

▌ Sister City Committee

Park, Recreation and Community Services Department | *Established 1925*

Aquatics, circa 1950.

The Burbank Park, Recreation and Community Services Department had two recreational facilities, ten parks, and a budget of $3,000 at its establishment in 1925. Today, the department manages forty-one parks and facilities, a public golf course, and a budget of over $14 million.

For more than eighty years, the department has played a key role in creating community and has prided itself in well-maintained recreational facilities; a wide variety of classes, events, and programs for participants of all ages; and access to special-interest activities such as volunteering, hiking, and golfing. Today, the Burbank Park, Recreation and Community Services Department has joined other communities in a message that Parks Make Life Better! It continues its unique dedication to improving and advancing service delivery and addressing the community's evolving recreational, social, and human-service needs.

Boards and Commissions Supported

▮ Art in Public Places Committee

▮ Child Care Committee

▮ Cultural Arts Commission

▮ Park, Recreation and Community Services Board

▮ Senior Citizen Board

▮ Youth Board

▮ Youth Endowment Services Fund Advisory Committee

Buena Vista Park story time. Photo courtesy of Burbank Historical Society, circa 1950.

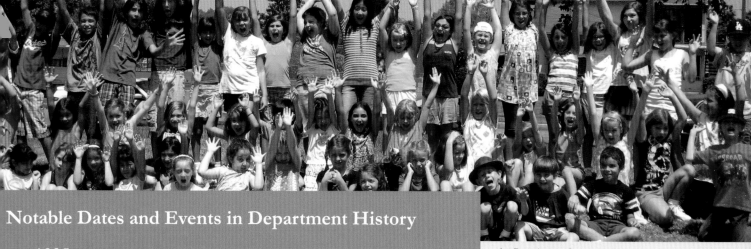

Notable Dates and Events in Department History

1925   The Park and Forestry Department and Commission is established. First park was dedicated, Vickroy Park.

1935   First scheduled performance in natural bowl amphitheater (Starlight Bowl).

1942   USO Headquarters (now Olive Recreation Center) to provide recreational services for military personnel and the community. Glenoaks Park (now McCambridge) is dedicated.

1946   Olive Memorial Baseball Stadium is dedicated.

1948   Verdugo Swimming Pool and bath house is completed.

1949-52   The St. Louis Browns professional baseball team utilizes Olive Memorial Stadium at Olive Avenue Park for spring training and exhibition games.

1950   The Park and Forestry Department and Playground and Recreation Department are consolidated into the Park and Recreation Board. First Civitan Day Parade and Baseball Jamboree held.

1951   Starlight Bowl is dedicated and features a live performance by the Burbank Symphony Orchestra.

1952   The Burbank Athletic Federation is founded to assist with oversight of sports programs.

1958-63   The Los Angeles Rams professional football team utilizes Olive Memorial Stadium for preseason training.

1959   DeBell Municipal Golf Course is dedicated.

1961   Verdugo Recreation Center is dedicated.

1969   Construction of War Memorial monument at McCambridge Park is completed.

1972   Joslyn Adult Center is dedicated. Retired Seniors Volunteer Program (RSVP) is also formed.

1989   Creative Arts Center at Izay Park is dedicated.

1993   The Art in Public Places Ordinance requires the provision of public art for development projects.

1997   Burbank Tennis Center is dedicated.

2001   Stough Canyon Nature Center is dedicated.

2009   Robert R. Ovrom Community Center and Park is dedicated.

Art Experiences Camp, 2010.

Girls softball, circa 1950. Photo courtesy of Burbankia.

McCambridge Park, teens around piano. Photo courtesy of Burbank Historical Society.

DeBell Municipal Golf Course

Police Department | *Established 1911*

Boards and Commissions Supported

| Police Commission

The Police Department works in partnership with the community to achieve positive impacts on crime and traffic and to provide professional police service in an ethical and courteous manner. The department provides services through four divisions: Patrol, Investigation, Administrative Services, and Special Operations.

Police radar unit.

Police break up an illegal still on Scott Road, 1922. Photo courtesy of Burbank Historical Society.

Burbank police, 1938.

Animal Shelter was built in 1952.

Notable Dates and Events in Department History

1911   The City Marshal's Office is established.

1914   Burbank voters approve a prohibition on alcohol in the City, setting the stage for moonshiners to begin operation.

1923   The City Marshal's Office becomes the Police Department.

1927   Burbank opens its first dog pound (animal shelter).

1948   Officers are hired to begin investigating establishments with illegal slot machines and other gambling paraphernalia.

1951   The Burbank Citizens Crime Prevention Committee is formed to investigate the presence of "syndicated crime" in Burbank.

1953   The Animal Commission is formed.

1957   The police horse auxiliary force is formed to patrol the hill and canyon areas.

1961   The new City Hall Annex (later renamed the Police Services Building) is completed at the corner of Olive Avenue and Third Street to house the Police Department and Civil Defense program.

1970   The ride-along program begins to allow citizens to ride along with police officers on patrol.

1973   Burbank Community Radio Watch, a group of band radio operators, is formed to help police combat crime.

1979   Burbank and Glendale form the Joint Attack on Burglary Program, which includes creation of the aerial support helicopter program.

1970s   The team policing concept is instituted with the creation of the police cadet program, School Resource Officer program, Impact (now DARE) program, and police chaplain program.

1980   Canine unit is established with two fully trained police dogs and their handlers.

1990s   Various new programs are established including bike patrol, the park ranger program, *Street Beat* weekly television program, and Special Response Team.

1990   The new Animal Shelter opens on Victory Place.

1998   The new Police/Fire Headquarters building opens at the corner of Orange Grove Avenue and Third Street.

Public Works Department | *Established 1911*

Engineers in old City Hall, circa 1940.

The Public Works Department plans, designs, builds, operates, and maintains the City's public works systems. These services are provided through six divisions: Administration, Engineering Design & Construction, Traffic, Fleet & Building Maintenance, Street & Sanitation, and Water Reclamation & Sewer. The Public Works Department's responsibilities include coordinating the design and construction of the City's major new municipal facilities; maintaining and repairing City equipment and buildings; performing or overseeing all work in the public right-of-way; designing and constructing streets and alleys; designing and installing traffic signs, signals, and other traffic management systems; constructing and maintaining the sewer system; street sweeping; and refuse collection. The Public Works Department operates the Water Reclamation Plan, Recycling Center, Landfill, City warehouse, and yard.

Refuse truck at Burbank Landfill.

Boards and Commissions Supported

▌ Traffic Commission

▌ Sustainable Burbank Task Force

Paving the 500 block of Clark Avenue, 1950.

Notable Dates and Events in Department History

Proposed capital improvement, 1954 bond.

1911 San Fernando Boulevard is the first street in the city to be paved.

1916 The first City Hall is constructed at Olive Avenue and Third Street (across from the current City Hall).

1920 Municipal garbage pick-up service begins.

1921 The first stop signs in Burbank are installed at the intersection of San Fernando and Olive.

1922 Outhouses are banned in Burbank.

1935 Burbank begins operating its own rock crushing and asphalt plant for street paving.

1939 Burbank purchases its first street sweeper and begins sweeping streets twice weekly.

1941 An underpass is built beneath the railroad along San Fernando Boulevard to eliminate the "Turkey Crossing" at-grade crossing at Victory Place and Empire Avenue.

1942 The Alameda and Olive Avenue bridges over the Burbank Flood Control Channel open.

1943 The new City Hall building opens across from the old City Hall.

1946 The first parking meters are installed in Downtown Burbank.

1949 The City landfill opens in the Verdugo Mountains.

1956 Trash incinerators are outlawed.

1958 The Olive Avenue overpass opens.

1959 The Magnolia Boulevard overpass opens.

1961 The Burbank Boulevard overpass opens.

The Golden State Freeway opens through Burbank; U.S. Route 99 along San Fernando Boulevard is decommissioned.

1962 The Ventura Freeway opens through Burbank; the State Route 134 designation is removed from Alameda Avenue.

1966 The Municipal Services Building opens behind City Hall; it was demolished in 2001 after being damaged in the 1994 Northridge Earthquake.

The Water Reclamation Plant is completed.

1982 The City's first recycle center opens on Chestnut Street.

2003 The Compressed Natural Gas fueling station opens for City vehicles and the public.

2006 The City's demonstration hydrogen fueling station opens for City vehicles.

The Burbank Boulevard bridge widening and Five Points intersection realignment projects are completed.

2008 The Burbank Boulevard streetscape project is completed.

Burbank's sustainability program is initiated with the adoption of the Sustainability Action Plan.

John Muir Middle School. Photo courtesy of Burbank Historical Society.

[Chapter Three]

Education

Burbank Unified School District

The Providencia School District was established in 1879. Dr. David Burbank donated the land to build the first school on Burbank Boulevard near what is now Mariposa Street.

In 1887, the newly formed town of Burbank saw a small spurt of new development. To accommodate an increase in residents, the Providencia School District replaced the grammar school with a two-story wood-framed grammar school building on Magnolia Boulevard near San Fernando Boulevard (which has since been demolished).

In order to meet the demands of the growing population, a two-story brick building, the Burbank Union High School, was constructed in 1909 at the northwest corner of Cypress Avenue and Second Street.

In 1919, Burbank Grammar School was replaced with Thomas A. Edison School located on San Fernando Boulevard. The original Burbank Union High School later became John Muir Junior High School. John Muir was replaced by a new junior high school, Burbank Junior High School (later named John Muir Junior High School), in 1924.

Burbank High School was constructed in 1922. The school opened in September, with a student body of three hundred and a faculty of twenty. A library was added to the original

Top: Union High School, 1909.
Bottom: Burbank Grammar School, 1903.
Photos courtesy of Burbank Historical Society.

building shortly after the school opened. By 1925, a swimming pool, industrial education shops, and tennis courts were added to enrich the instructional program.

The 1920s would be a period of growth for Burbank schools. From 1922 to 1923, Abraham Lincoln and Joaquin Miller Schools opened their doors, and a new school building replaced the original Edison School. Burbank voters passed a school bond in 1924, resulting in McKinley, Roosevelt, and Washington Elementary Schools being built. These schools opened in 1926. That same year, John Burroughs Junior High School was completed and would later become a senior high school in 1948.

In 1928, the Burbank Union School District and Elementary City School District were unified, with the creation of a Board of Education and the addition of a school superintendent.

Burbank's population growth during World War II was a precursor to the post-war boom period. The growth resulted in the construction of new elementary schools during the war. These were Thomas A. Edison School (1940), Bret Harte School (1941), and Monterey School and Henry M. Mingay School (1945). In 1941, Central Elementary School also opened. In 1969, the school was re-named Walt Disney Elementary School.

Post–World War II, there would be another period of growth for Burbank schools. In 1948, four new schools opened—Jefferson and Stevenson Elementary Schools, and Jordan and Luther Burbank Junior High Schools.

With more children in the city during the post-war period, new schools were constructed to relieve the overcrowding at existing ones. Schools constructed during this period were Providencia Elementary School (1952) and Horace Mann School (1955). In 1952, John Muir Junior High School relocated from its 1924 location to its current location in the Benmar Hills residential area at Kenneth and Delaware roads.

Burbank High School

John Burroughs High School

St. Finbar School

Shortly after opening Saint Joseph Hospital, the Sisters of Providence opened a new elementary school in the neighboring St. Finbar Parish. The first classes were held in large open tents and in the church until construction of the school was completed in 1945. Sisters of Providence continued to teach at the school until 1984.

Top: St. Finbar School. Photo courtesy of St. Finbar School.

Top Right: St. Finbar charter class as ninth graders in 1945. Photo courtesy of St. Finbar School.

Middle Left: Providence High School classes were held in tents when the school opened in 1955. Photo courtesy of Providence High School.

Bottom Left: Graduating class of 1965. Photo courtesy of Providence High School.

Bottom Right: Providence High School students, circa 1960. Photo courtesy of Providence High School.

Providence High School

In 1955, the Sisters of Providence opened Providence High School for girls. First classes were taught in donated circus tents in the parking lot until a permanent structure was completed later that fall. In 1974, Providence would become a coeducational institution with the inclusion of boys. Since that time, Providence has enjoyed continuous accreditation by the Western Association of Schools and Colleges.

St. Robert Bellarmine School

St. Robert Bellarmine Parish was first known as Holy Trinity Parish and established in 1907. The school opened in 1936 and had a total of eighty-eight students. It was staffed by Five Sisters, members of the Sisters of Charity of the Blessed Virgin Mary. In 1938, the school was renamed St. Robert Bellarmine.

Top Left: Holy Trinity Church before 1940. Photo courtesy of St. Robert Bellarmine Grammar School.

Middle Left: First high school building, 1950. Photo courtesy of St. Robert Bellarmine Grammar School.

Middle Right: St. Robert Bellarmine Grammar School students, 1946. Photo courtesy of St. Robert Bellarmine Grammar School.

Bottom Inset: Bellarmine-Jefferson High School, 1962. Photo courtesy of Burbank Historical Society.

Bottom: Bellarmine-Jefferson High School football practice 1949. Photo courtesy of Bellarmine-Jefferson High School.

Bellarmine-Jefferson High School

The cornerstone of the first wing of Bellarmine-Jefferson High School was laid in 1945 and an addition was completed in 1950. The auditorium was added in 1954 and the gymnasium in 1982.

The school was named after both St. Robert Bellarmine and Thomas Jefferson to express the commonly held ideals of both. St. Robert Bellarmine (1542–1621) was an Italian Jesuit and Cardinal whose views, as expressed in his writings, agreed in many aspects with the views of Thomas Jefferson (1743–1826), author of the Declaration of Independence, and later president of the United States.

Top: St. Francis Xavier School. Photo courtesy of St. Francis Xavier School.

Bottom: American Lutheran School.

St. Francis Xavier School

Established in the 1950s, St. Francis Xavier is a Catholic elementary school for students from kindergarten through junior high school.

American Lutheran School

American Lutheran Church opened in 1941. The congregation founded American Lutheran Elementary School in 1946 and continued to offer a quality academic education in a Christian environment for sixty years, until its closure at the end of the 2006 school year.

First Lutheran School

First Lutheran School Burbank is a private Christian school located on the border of Glendale and Burbank. First Lutheran has been serving the educational and spiritual needs of elementary school children in the Burbank, Glendale, and Los Angeles areas since 1950.

Top: Villa Cabrini Orphanage Campus.
Right: Entrance to Villa Cabrini Academy.
Photos courtesy of Woodbury University.

Woodbury University

In 1910, Mother Frances Xavier Cabrini purchased a 475-acre parcel of the Rancho San Rafael land. In 1912, Mother Cabrini, with the Missionary Sisters of the Sacred Heart of Jesus, opened an orphanage and preventorium for children at risk for acquiring tuberculosis.

The property was later divided into tracts for homes, businesses, and churches. In 1933, the orphanage transitioned into what would become Villa Cabrini Academy, an all-girls Catholic boarding school. By this point Mother Cabrini had been canonized as America's first Saint.

In 1968, the Academy closed and the property was leased to California Institute for the Arts (now located in Valencia).

In the 1970s, the property was sold to Cal Lutheran High School. In 1985, Woodbury University acquired a portion of the Cabrini property. Two years later, the students and faculty moved from Los Angeles to the Burbank campus.

Woodbury Business College was a landmark business college established in 1884 by Francis Chute Woodbury. For 104 years, the campus was located in central Los Angeles on Wilshire Boulevard.

Since the move to Burbank, Woodbury has made many campus improvements, rehabilitating older buildings, and

Top: Woodbury's new School of Business building, made possible by donations to the $27 million Building Initiative.

Left: Entrance to Woodbury University.

Right: Woodbury University commencement, Class of 2010.

Photos courtesy of Woodbury University.

constructing modern-style buildings, including the George Isaacs Faculty Center. The university has been squarely on the path for growth in academic quality, in particular with the addition of new programs such as architecture and animation.

Under the guidance of current president, Dr. Kenneth R. Nielsen, Woodbury's mission to educate and prepare its students to be vital and relevant global citizens, while maintaining national prosperity, will endure. From the beginning, no Woodbury student was ever encouraged to think small . . . and now, as this innovative institution of higher learning moves into the future, it has shaken off the dust of the past to forge ahead toward the promise to turn eager learners into innovative leaders.

Alumni

Clockwise from top left:

Tim Matheson	John Burroughs High School	Actor, director, producer
Ron Howard	John Burroughs High School	Director, producer, actor
Tim Burton	Burbank High School	Director, producer
Debbie Reynolds	Burbank High School & John Burroughs High School	Actor, singer, entertainer
Cathy Ferguson	Burbank High School	Olympic Gold Medalist
Laura Ziskin	Burbank High School	Writer, producer
Helen Hunt	Providence High School	Actor
Blake Lively	Burbank High School	Actor

Alumni

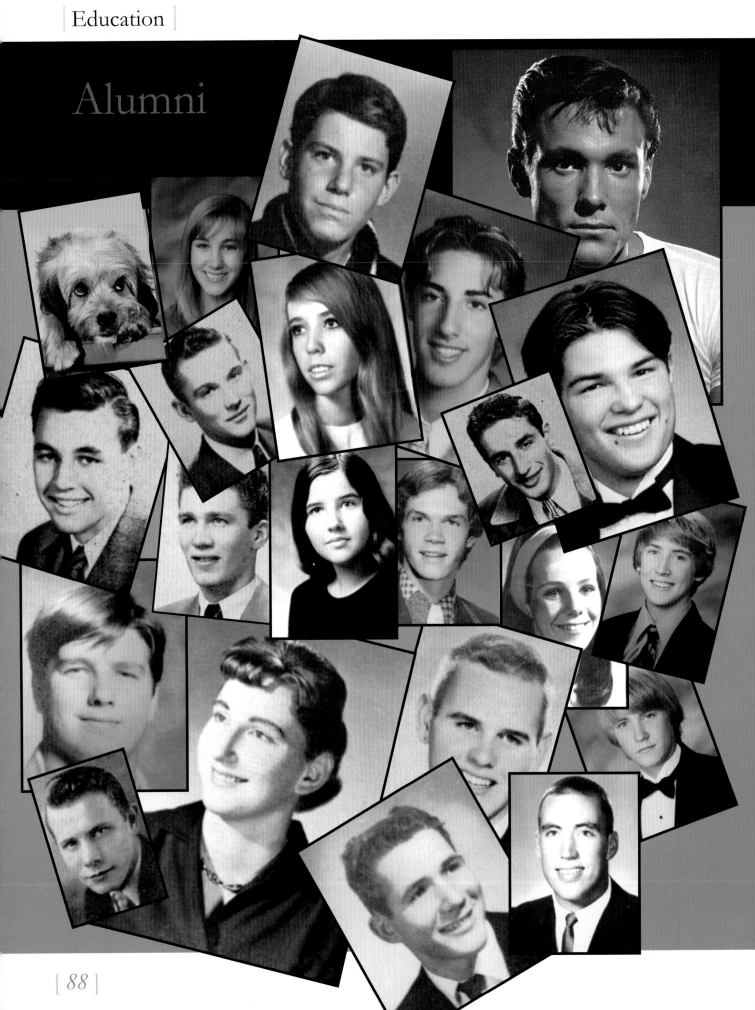

Alumni pictured at left:

Row One:

Benji the Dog	Burbank Animal Shelter	Actor
Natasha Wynnyk	Burbank High School	Actor
Anson Williams	Burbank High School	Actor
William Smith	Burbank High School	Actor

Row Two:

Boyd Browne	Burbank High School	President, Mattel
Frank Sullivan	Burbank High School	MLB player
Melissa Mathison	Providence High School	Screenwriter
Eric Balfour	John Burroughs High School	Actor, singer
Vic Tayback	Burbank High School	Actor
Freddy Sanchez	Burbank High School	MLB player

Row Three:

Paul Cameron	Burbank High School	NFL player
Melody Scott Thomas	Providence High School	Actor
Mitch Vogel	Burbank High School	Actor
Marta Waller	Providence High School	News anchor
Dylan Tuomy Wilhoit	John Burroughs High School	Actor

Row Four:

Mike McDonald	John Burroughs High School	NFL player
Linda Murphy	John Burroughs High School	Olympic Volleyball Player
Maynard Michael Parker	Burbank High School	Actor
Blake Tuomy Wilhoit	John Burroughs High School	Actor

Row Five:

Arnold Peterson	Burbank High School	Co-founder Bob's Big Boy
Ron Morris	John Burroughs High School	Olympic Pole Vaulter
Lynn Shackelford	John Burroughs High School	ABA player, LA Laker broadcaster

Attendees of Burbank schools not pictured

Kelly Blatz	Actor
Angela Cartwright	Actor
Veronica Cartwright	Actor
Tiffany Chin	Olympic Figure Skater
Jeff Cirillo	MLB player
Josie Davis	Actor
Angie Dickinson (Brown)	Actor
Debbie Dunning	Actor, model
David Faustino	Actor
Lindsay Felton	Actor
Kim Fields	Actor
Jaimee Foxworthy	Actor
Kenneth Friedkin	Founder, Pacific Southwest Airlines
Seychelle Gabriel	Actor
Darlene Gillespie	Mouseketeer
Dave Goelz	Muppets performer, creator of Gonzo
Don Grady (Agrati)	Actor
Gary Grimes	Actor
Dan Haggerty	Actor
Allen Hall	Actor
Jennifer Love Hewitt	Actor
Chuck Hicks	Stunt actor
Clint Howard	Actor
Jamie Jaffe	Producer
Ashley Johnson	Actor
Michael Kirst	Actor
Erik Kramer	NFL player
DeDe Lind	Model
Kristy McNichol	Actor
Mike Magnante	MLB player
Erin Moran	Actor
Brittany Murphy	Actor
Jairo Penaranda	NFL player
Randy Rhoads	Guitarist for Ozzie Osbourne
Renee Russo	Actor
Beverly Adams Sassoon	Actor, publisher, Sassoon products
Jenna Boyd Stevenson	Actor
Mena Suvari	Actor
Doreen Tracey	Mousketeer
Michelle Trachtenberg	Actor
Leon Tyler	Actor
Mara Wilson	Actor
Elijah Wood	Actor
Ralph "Donald Zink" Woods	Actor

California Admissions Day Centennial Parade with Hopalong Cassidy on horseback. Photo courtesy of Burbank Historical Society.

Chapter Four

Community Organizations

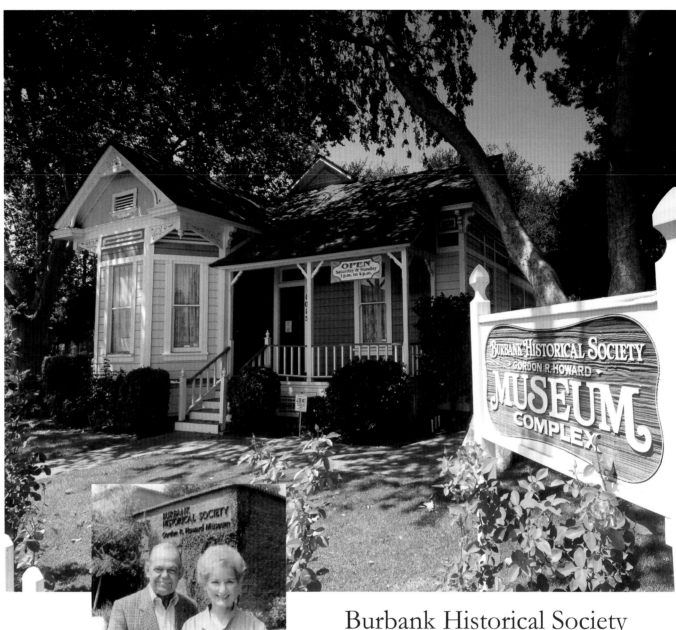

Top: Restored 1887 frame Victorian house, one of the six original houses built by the Providencia Land, Water and Development Company.

Inset: The late Gordon R. Howard and Burbank Historical Society founder Mary Jane Strickland, 1984.

Photos courtesy of Burbank Historical Society.

Burbank Historical Society

The Burbank Historical Society was founded in 1973 and incorporated in 1975. Members are committed to collecting and preserving the rich history of the Burbank community. The Gordon R. Howard Museum was named in honor of major benefactors, Gordon and Mary Howard. The museum is located in George Izay Park and includes the Historical Society's historical and antique collection and the 1887 Victorian house.

Boys & Girls Club of Burbank and Greater East Valley

The mission of the Boys & Girls Club of Burbank and Greater East Valley is to inspire and enable all young people to realize their full potential as productive, responsible, and caring citizens. The club has a distinguished fifteen-year history operating a main branch and twelve satellite campuses that serve more than 850 youth a day. When the school day comes to a close, the club opens its doors to a positive place. Most importantly, no child is turned away for an inability to pay. Over 60 percent of members receive scholarships to participate.

Right: Boys & Girls Club of Burbank.

Bottom: BCR participants at Burbank on Parade.

Burbank Center for the Retarded (BCR)

In 1963, the Burbank Center for the Retarded (BCR) opened its doors at the First Congregational Church of Burbank as a day program serving adults with developmental disabilities. Today, BCR provides a safe, structured, and caring environment where adults and pre-school through school-aged participants are valued, accepted, and understood. BCR continues to proudly serve, offering a supportive environment and providing key programming for its participants.

Triumphant crew of the Hill-Davis streamliner.

61 CITY OF BURBANK JUNIOR CHAMBER · COMMERCE

Top: The Walt Disney Studios bridge over Riverside Drive.

Left: Burbank Junior Chamber of Commerce.

Burbank Chamber of Commerce

The Burbank Chamber of Commerce was established in 1920 and is considered today to be the leading business advocate within the city, promoting economic growth and prosperity, serving as a vital strategic partner in initiatives that enhance and preserve the quality of life within our community, and providing valued services to our diverse business members. According to the *Los Angeles Business Journal*, the Burbank Chamber of Commerce is currently the fourteenth largest chamber out of eighty-nine in Los Angeles County when it comes to overall revenue for 2010, and is the eighth largest chamber when it comes to actual total member businesses.

The Burbank Chamber of Commerce represents nearly 1,000 member businesses with more than 33,000 employees. They welcome new businesses into the chamber family and look forward to providing valuable advocacy, programs, discounts, and promotional opportunities that enhance the value of chamber membership. The Burbank Chamber of Commerce strives "to be the leading public policy advocate for business; to promote economic growth; to be a strategic partner in initiatives that enhance and preserve the quality of life in the Burbank community; and to provide valued services to our members."

Top: Burbank Community YMCA, circa 1945.
Inset: Current Burbank Community YMCA.

Burbank Community YMCA

In 1924, the Burbank Community YMCA was established and chartered by local citizens, making it the oldest nonprofit in the city. In 1932, it was able to purchase the present property from the First Baptist Church. Herbert Hoover was president, the country was in the midst of the Great Depression, and people needed a place to come together. They came to the Y.

With a mission *"to provide people of all ages lifelong opportunities to become stronger in spirit, mind and body,"* the Y currently supports more than 18,000 members. The Y's breadth and scope of expertise includes wellness, physical fitness, child development, and leadership programs. In its eighty-sixth year of service, the Y has been the "only place" for four generations of families, and aspires to be that place for the next four generations.

Burbank Coordinating Council

Since 1933, the Burbank Coordinating Council (BCC) has brought together representatives from both the public and private sectors to promote the health and welfare of youth and adults. BCC supported ideas that grew into key programs such as Burbank Temporary Aid Center, school crossing guards, senior and youth boards, and the Holiday Basket program. The group continuously meets with schools, faith-based organizations, the City, service clubs, businesses, and individuals to insure a better tomorrow for Burbank.

Burbank Housing Corporation

Burbank Housing Corporation's (BHC) vision statement is *Life Enrichment Through Neighborhood Improvement*. Incorporated in 1997, the organization's mission is to preserve, upgrade, and develop affordable housing opportunities in Burbank and to provide a safe, service-enriched environment for residents in their communities. BHC's mission aligns with the City Redevelopment Agency, particularly with a dedication to removing blight, strengthening community in partnership with residents, and presenting valuable opportunities for involvement.

Burbank Ministerial Association

The Burbank Ministerial Association (BMA) is the only organization that exists in Burbank to provide networking and input on the many services and concerns of which those in the faith community all have need. The Ministerial Association addresses the personal life of the pastor; issues before the City of Burbank; and the health, psychological care, and human issues of community members on a regular basis. The organization also cooperates with and supports projects and programs that improve quality of life in the community.

Burbank on Parade

To celebrate the conclusion of World War II in 1945, the Burbank Junior Chamber of Commerce organized a city parade and spring festival. The community embraced the festivities, and the extravaganza became very successful. Events were scheduled throughout the week and included a pageant, dances, bake contests, and a carnival. The parade and festival became an annual tradition that continued for the next twelve years.

In 1981, a group of Burbank residents revived the tradition of celebrating hometown spirit. In lieu of a weeklong festival, the group opted to plan an annual spring parade to celebrate community pride. For nearly thirty years, the parade has featured a grand marshal, decorated floats, marching bands, antique and vintage cars, equestrians, novelties, and special Burbank VIPs. Past grand marshals have included actors and celebrities Andy Griffith, Vic Tayback, Johnny Grant, Donald O'Connor, Alan Hale, Jo Anne Worley, Debbie Reynolds, George Lopez, and Anson Williams.

Burbank Temporary Aid Center

In 1974, the Burbank Ministerial Association and Burbank Coordinating Council recognized the need for a centralized source of services for the less fortunate in the community. The Burbank Temporary Aid Center (BTAC) was founded to provide the poor, working poor, and homeless of the local community with basic services necessary to live with dignity, and to serve citizens of Burbank in times of emergency and disaster. BTAC strives to help create a community where the poor and working poor are able to access necessary resources and services to move from poverty to self-sufficiency. BTAC provides assistance to more than 7,000 individuals or families of all ethnic and religious backgrounds annually.

Top: BTAC facility located on West Burbank Boulevard.

Middle Left: Burbank City Employees Association entry for Burbank on Parade, 1950.

Middle Right: Burbank on Parade, circa 1940.

Bottom: Burbank on Parade with actor and rodeo star Montie Montana riding on horseback, 1949.

Burbank Tournament of Roses Association

From the early days, the Burbank community has coordinated efforts to design and build a float for the prestigious Pasadena Tournament of Roses Parade. In 1914, Burbank's first entry was titled "Goddess of Plenty." Parade officials were so impressed that they awarded the float the Special Prize—Second Place Silver Cup.

Since 1914, some of the most beautiful entries were constructed and decorated by volunteers from civic organizations such as the Burbank Chamber of Commerce, Burbank Schools, and Junior Chamber of Commerce. Among the entries were the 1938 float, "Merry-Go-Round," and the 1939 entry, "Tally-Ho of 1889." Both of these floats earned Burbank the prestigious Sweepstakes Trophy.

Burbank's first entry in the Pasadena Tournament of Roses Parade, 1914. City's first float rider, Miss Stella Hansen, a high school teacher. Float Photos Courtesy Tournament of Roses Archives. Trophy Photo by Erik C. Andersen.

© Pasadena Tournament of Roses

© Pasadena Tournament of Roses

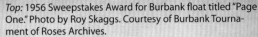

Top: 1956 Sweepstakes Award for Burbank float titled "Page One." Photo by Roy Skaggs. Courtesy of Burbank Tournament of Roses Archives.

Middle: 1961 Sweepstakes Award for Burbank float titled "Orchids in the Moonlight." Photo by Roy Skaggs. Courtesy of Burbank Tournament of Roses Archives.

Bottom: 2011 Founder's Trophy for the "Most Spectacular Built and Decorated by Volunteers from a Community or Organization" for Burbank float titled "Centennial Celebration," designed by Julio Leon. Photo by Erik C. Andersen.

In 1946, the Burbank Tournament of Roses Association (BTORA) was formed, and once again Burbank submitted an entry in the parade. The organization was comprised completely of community volunteers. In sixty-five years, the dedicated efforts of BTORA have led to twenty-two major awards, including three Sweepstakes Trophies.

In keeping with the tradition of community spirit, BTORA honored the City of Burbank's one hundred-year anniversary with the 2011 Rose Float entry titled "Centennial Celebration." The centennial float not only represented Burbank in Pasadena's epic parade, but it also reflected the dedication and civic pride of the Burbank community.

Family Promise

Family Promise of the East San Fernando Valley is a nonprofit formed in 2008 by congregants of various faith communities in the Burbank/Glendale area. Family Promise helps mobilize communities to provide safe shelter, meals, and support services for homeless families. It provides an interfaith network of support and maintains a goal of helping families regain housing independence. The organization opened its doors to offer housing assistance to families in the summer of 2010. It partnered with Burbank Housing Corporation and the City to secure a location for a day center where families work with social workers to get back into independent living.

Top right: Annual Family Promise fund-raiser Cardboard Box City, 2009.

Middle: Family Services Agency.

Bottom: Dental clinic services.

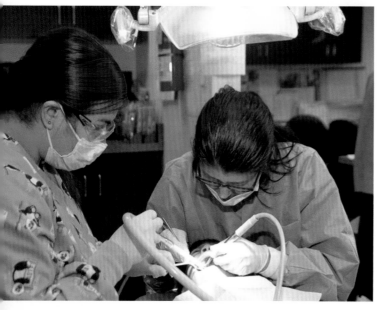

Family Service Agency of Burbank

Since 1953, the Family Service Agency of Burbank (FSA) has responded to the community's expressed needs by providing a wide range of low-to-no-cost community-based counseling and social services designed to address the clinical, psycho-educational, and residential needs of the Burbank community. A core belief of FSA's leadership remains that a strong community can only be built where there are healthy youth, adults, couples, and families.

After more than fifty-five years of critical community service, FSA was able to move to a new facility, expanding services to meet growing needs. FSA offers many programs including parenting, art therapy, teen anger management, and a partnership-founded school-based counseling program. The agency's ever-present goal is to "build a better community, one family at a time."

Kids' Community Dental Clinic

The Kids' Community Dental Clinic mission is to provide affordable, quality dental care to children of low-income families with no access to insurance or other coverage. A children's dental clinic existed in Burbank for more than thirty years through the generosity of the Sisters of Providence Saint Joseph Medical Center. When the hospital dental clinic closed in 1997, many parents had a difficult time finding low-cost dental care. In 2002, with strong support from the City of Burbank, clinic doors re-opened at the Burbank Community YMCA. In 2008, in partnership with the Burbank Unified School District, the clinic relocated to its current location on the McKinley Elementary campus. The clinic provides low-cost treatment to children from all over Southern California, ages eighteen and younger, and has built and sustained a reputation for three strong programs: in-clinic dental treatments, school screenings, and public health fair event screenings. The Kids' Community Dental Clinic is clearly thriving, providing more than 2,000 dental treatments in 2009.

Leadership Burbank

Leadership Burbank offers a nine-month leadership program training leaders and emerging leaders in the city. The mission of Leadership Burbank is to identify, educate, and motivate current and emerging leaders to develop ideas and solutions that make Burbank a strong, sustainable, and vibrant community. It was founded by the Burbank Chamber of Commerce, City of Burbank, Burbank Unified School District, and Woodbury University.

Neighborhood Leadership Program

In 2008, a grassroots Neighborhood Leadership Program was established to enhance Connect with Your Community objectives and build long-term social health. In partnership with the Burbank Unified School District and Leadership Burbank and through educational and tool-based programming, the program's objectives are to make residents resource experts, increase neighborhood ownership, and inspire leadership by engaging residents to actively develop and promote community programs. Ultimately, the sustainable goal of the program is for graduates to independently create, empower, and sustain neighborhoods with the valuable tools and support they have acquired.

Top: Burbank "B" on the hill was restored by the Leadership Burbank, 2010. Photo courtesy of Leadership Burbank.

Middle: Mt. View Park Beautification Project, Leadership Burbank, 2004. Photo courtesy of Leadership Burbank.

Bottom: Neighborhood Leadership Program. Photo courtesy of Andre Murray.

Providence Saint Joseph Medical Center

Nearly seventy years ago, a vision began taking shape to build a community hospital that would bring quality medical care to the small but illustrious City of Burbank. That vision materialized as Providence Saint Joseph Medical Center (formally St. Joseph Hospital).

St. Joseph Hospital was built on eleven acres of ranchland donated by Lockheed Aircraft Corporation, one of the pillars of Burbank. The hospital was founded in 1943 by the Sisters of Providence. More than 3,000 people attended the dedication ceremony. Burbank's landmark studios were instrumental in building the hospital. The Walt Disney Studios, Warner Bros., and NBC Studios helped finance the initial construction and continued to help over the years as the hospital expanded. In 2010, led by the Roy and Patricia Disney family, the entertainment industry contributed more than $15 million to the newest addition: the state-of-the-art Roy and Patricia Disney Family Cancer Center. The community also contributed, making this center the most comprehensive cancer diagnostic and treatment facility in the area.

Providence Saint Joseph Medical Center has a long history of providing high-quality care for the community. The Hospital is proud to continue serving the mission of its founders and aims to continue for generations to come.

Today, the landmark Providence Saint Joseph Medical Center has developed far beyond the dreams of the Sisters of Providence to become one of the top hospitals in the region. But even as Providence Saint Joseph has more than quadrupled in size and stepped up as a leader in top medical technology, the mission of its founders to serve the poor and vulnerable with high-quality and compassionate care has not changed.

Top: Groundbreaking ceremony for the Providence Saint Joseph Medical Center in 1943. Archbishop J.F.A. McIntyre officiated at the event, which was attended by church officials, the Sisters of Charity of the House of Providence, Walt Disney, and other invited guests.

Bottom: In the mid-1990s, the Sisters of Providence Health System, which owns St. Joseph in Burbank, renamed the hospital Providence Saint Joseph Medical Center.

Photos courtesy of Providence Saint Joseph Medical Center.

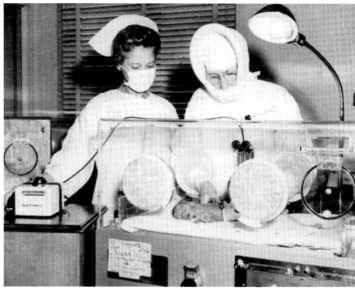

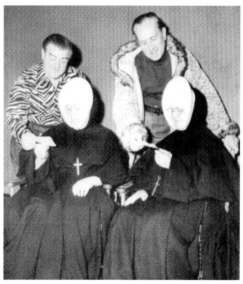

Top Right: Nursery, 1960.

Middle Right: Comedy duo Bud Abbott and Lou Costello present Sisters Agnes and Zephirin with donations for construction of the new hospital, 1951.

Left: Roy and Patricia Disney Family Cancer Center is the largest provider of cancer services in the region, offering diagnosis, treatment, professional counseling, access to support groups, and educational resources in one healing environment.

Photos courtesy of Providence Saint Joseph Medical Center.

Road Kings

The Road Kings of Burbank is a notable car club that raced and toured throughout the United States. Ralph Marshall and Dave Osterkamp established the Road Kings in Burbank in 1952, and the club became one of drag racing's all-time recognized car clubs. From the 1950s through the 1960s, some of the preeminent members included nationally recognized drag racers like the Cedarquist brothers, Tommy Ivo, Don "the Snake" Prudhomme, Ken Safford, Jim Miles, and Bob Muravez. Today, the Burbank Road Kings continue to be dedicated to charitable efforts, participate in parades and picnics, and coordinate annual car shows in the community.

Top: Road Kings and NHRA Hall of Fame member Don "the Snake" Prudhomme.

Middle Left: During a photo shoot for *Hot Rod* magazine on the set of his television show, *Road King* member Tommy "T.V." Ivo stands behind one of his ground-breaking dragsters. Ivo was inducted into the National Hot Rod Association (NHRA) Hall of Fame in 2005. Photo courtesy of the Tommy Ivo Collection.

Middle Right: Teen campaign volunteers and Salvation Army plan for 1962 "Crusade for Mercy's Sake."

Salvation Army of Burbank

The Salvation Army Burbank Corps opened its doors in 1957. The Salvation Army, an international movement, is an evangelical part of the universal Christian Church. Its message is based on the Bible, and its ministry is motivated by the love of God meeting human needs without discrimination. A volunteer-based Advisory Board of notable leaders representing various community sectors has guided the mission of the organization. The Salvation Army of Burbank is proud of its many services and programs, including its Youth Corps, Women's Ministries, Sunday services, successful Kettle Campaign, annual food and toy drive, and Thanksgiving Dinner.

Service Clubs

Service and volunteerism have been an integral part of the Burbank community throughout the years. Many service clubs and organizations have provided its members with opportunities to contribute and give back. From assisting with special events to helping the mentally and physically disabled, from working with animals to contributing to our schools, the people who make up these clubs make life in Burbank truly special.

Religious Organizations

American Lutheran Church

American Lutheran Church held its first worship service in 1941. In the early years, many of those who joined the congregation were Lutherans who came to the Burbank area during World War II to work for Lockheed Aircraft.

Burbank First United Methodist Church

Burbank First United Methodist Church was dedicated in 1884 on the site of what is now the Empire Center. Four years after that dedication, the church moved to San Fernando Boulevard where it remained until moving to Third Street and Olive Avenue in 1922. Continuing to grow, the current church location on Glenoaks Boulevard was completed in 1952.

Burbank First Presbyterian Church

Burbank First Presbyterian Church was built in 1888 at Fifth Street and Palm Avenue and was used until it was leveled by a windstorm in 1891. A new church was completed in 1894 at Third Street and Angeleno Avenue and was used until it was destroyed by fire in 1915. Another church was constructed at Fifth Street and Olive Avenue, which remains the present location.

Burbank Little White Chapel Christian Church

The Disciples of Christ opened the Little White Chapel in 1941.

Chapel on the Hill

Mother Cabrini helped build a one-room Marian Chapel at Villa Cabrini in 1917. The building rested in the hills above the Villa Cabrini campus and was visible from the San Fernando Valley basin. The chapel was later moved and is now located at St. Francis Xavier Church.

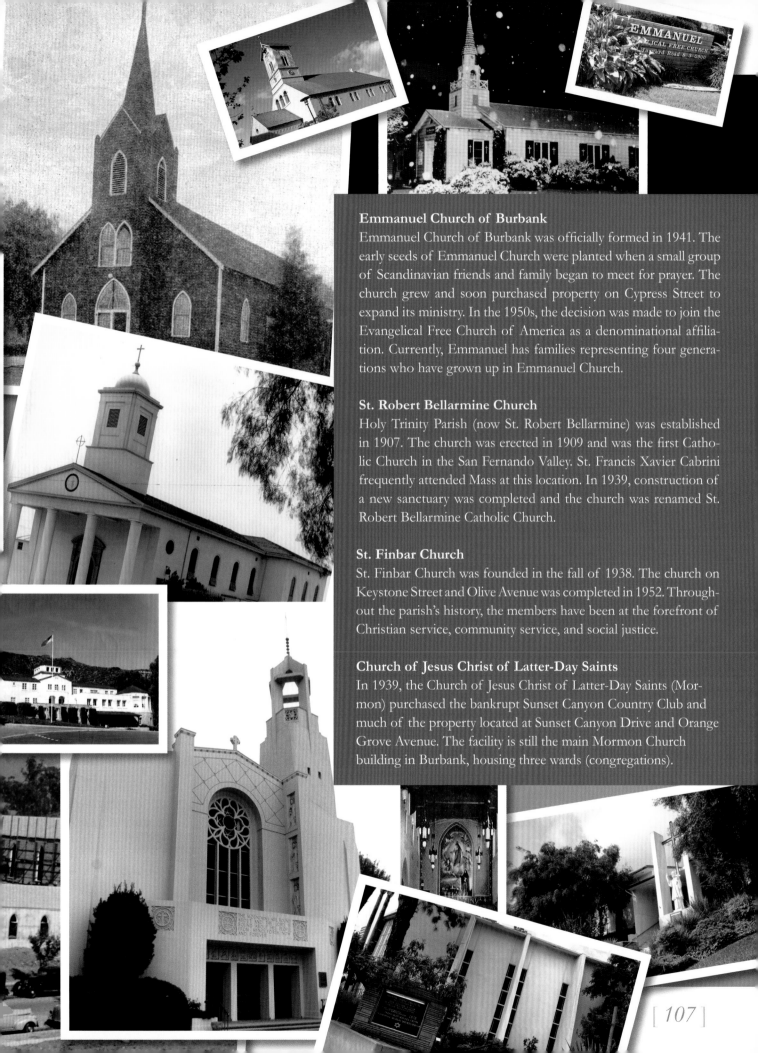

Emmanuel Church of Burbank

Emmanuel Church of Burbank was officially formed in 1941. The early seeds of Emmanuel Church were planted when a small group of Scandinavian friends and family began to meet for prayer. The church grew and soon purchased property on Cypress Street to expand its ministry. In the 1950s, the decision was made to join the Evangelical Free Church of America as a denominational affiliation. Currently, Emmanuel has families representing four generations who have grown up in Emmanuel Church.

St. Robert Bellarmine Church

Holy Trinity Parish (now St. Robert Bellarmine) was established in 1907. The church was erected in 1909 and was the first Catholic Church in the San Fernando Valley. St. Francis Xavier Cabrini frequently attended Mass at this location. In 1939, construction of a new sanctuary was completed and the church was renamed St. Robert Bellarmine Catholic Church.

St. Finbar Church

St. Finbar Church was founded in the fall of 1938. The church on Keystone Street and Olive Avenue was completed in 1952. Throughout the parish's history, the members have been at the forefront of Christian service, community service, and social justice.

Church of Jesus Christ of Latter-Day Saints

In 1939, the Church of Jesus Christ of Latter-Day Saints (Mormon) purchased the bankrupt Sunset Canyon Country Club and much of the property located at Sunset Canyon Drive and Orange Grove Avenue. The facility is still the main Mormon Church building in Burbank, housing three wards (congregations).

Shift change at Lockheed Gate 8 on Hollywood Way, 1943. Photo courtesy of Lockheed Martin.

Chapter Five

Business in Burbank

Made in Burbank

Packaged landing gear for Lockheed's *Electra*

Score Another First for Menasco!

The nose and main landing gear produced by Menasco for the Lockheed Electra will be delivered as complete pre-tested, functional systems, ready for installation in the airframe. This includes tires, wheels, brakes, steering system, wiring, plumbing, gear-mounted valves and switches.

It is fitting, too, that the Electra, America's first turbo-prop airliner, utilizes the latest advance in landing gear design and manufacture — Uniwelding of high heat treat steels—a combination pioneered and offered exclusively by MENASCO, specialists in aircraft landing gear.

First in development, quality, delivery and service

menasco manufacturing company

805 South San Fernando Boulevard, Burbank, California

SPECIALISTS IN AIRCRAFT LANDING GEAR

JULY 16, 1956   Circle No. 17 on Reader Service Card.

BICYCLE AND AUTO
— REPAIRING —
LIGHT FIXTURES ....
SPORTING GOODS ....
PIPE - FITTING ...
O. C. LANE JR.

EL PORTANA

RAGE.

ESTD 1910

UNION SUPPLY CO.
POULTRY AND STOCK FEEDS

McKEON

BURBANK
YELLOW CLING PEACHES

BURBANK
YELLOW CLING PEACHES

Aeroq

THE 1928 COMPANY

Lockheed |

J une 15, 1913: A wood and fabric seaplane built in a garage made its first two flights over San Francisco Bay, inscribing a new name on the roll of aviation pioneers. Allan and Malcolm Loughead (pronounced and later spelled Lockheed) called their invention the Model G Hydro-Aeroplane. The ensuing years were dotted with many ups and downs for the Loughead brothers, ending with bankruptcy early in 1932.

June 6, 1932: Three young entrepreneurs rose from their seats in the federal courthouse in Los Angeles as Judge Harry Holzer entered and ascended the bench. Robert E. Gross, Carl B. Squier, and Lloyd C. Stearman were in the courtroom with a certified check in hand to rescue the bankrupt aircraft company. With scrutiny, the judge studied the only bid before him, accompanied by a certified check that offered to purchase the assets of the Lockheed company for $40,000. Holzer rapped his gavel, sealing the agreement, adding: "I hope you know what you are doing."

Top: Lockheed Plant B-1 in Burbank with tents. Note runway located on right side of picture.

Right: B-17 Flying Fortress, 1942. More than 2,700 B-17 bombers were produced during World War II by the Lockheed-owned Vega Company.

Photos courtesy of Lockheed Martin Photo.

Gross turned to the men beside him and quipped, "Now we can go to work." They shook hands and walked out into an economic picture of the gloomiest kind, as the United States was in the very depth of the most crippling depression ever experienced. The $40,000 investment gave them the right to negotiate a lease on an idle factory in Burbank, then a community of 16,000.

Out of that determination grew the Lockheed Aircraft Corporation, and from that modest seed grew an organization known throughout the world for many of the greatest aviation accomplishments.

December 7, 1941: The carnage and destruction that Japanese carrier planes reaped at Pearl Harbor brought about sudden, solid support for national defense. As a result, Lockheed's Burbank plant ramped up to nearly 94,000 employees over the next four years producing aircraft for the national defense including the Vega Ventura Patrol Bomber;

Top: Actress and model Frances Langford posing in front of March of Dimes nose art on a B-17.

Above: Lockheed Burbank Facility under camouflage during P-38 rollout, 1943.

Photos courtesy of Lockheed Martin Photo.

PV-1 and PV-2 Harpoons; the B-17 Flying Fortress; the Constellation—originally designed for commercial use, it was reconfigured as the C-69 military transport—and the XP-80, secretly designed by Kelly Johnson with a small, dedicated group of engineers, marking the beginning of the Lockheed Skunk Works®.

As the end of the Cold War approached, there was a sharp decline in national defense spending. After the C-5B, TR-1, P-3C, and F-117A were delivered and the SR-71 was retired, Lockheed began to consolidate manufacturing plants. In 1990, the board approved relocating plant operations from Burbank to Marietta, Georgia, and Skunk Works® to Palmdale, California. As a part of Lockheed Martin Aeronautics Company, the Skunk Works® continues to develop innovative solutions for the challenges of tomorrow.

Top: Thirty-five movie stars, reporters, and executives board a Constellation piloted by Howard Hughes for TWA's new daily nonstop service between Los Angeles and New York City. Descending from the top are Celeste Holm, Paulette Goddard, Veronica Lake, and Tom Conway, circa 1946.

Left: Lockheed Burbank Facility under Camouflage, 1943.

Photos courtesy of Lockheed Martin Photo.

Top Left: Actor Humphrey Bogart speaks with cadets at the Lockheed Air Terminal.

Top Right: Lockheed employees evacuate to bomb shelters for a drill, 1943.

Right: Grace Kelly, Liz Taylor, and Laraine Day boarding a TWA Constellation for a promo flight.

Photos courtesy of Lockheed Martin Photo.

Media Capital of the World

Since the Roaring Twenties, Burbank has experienced significant growth in commercial and real estate development. Burbank's legacy as the "Media Capital of the World" is supported through the location of the world's largest media companies right here in town, including Warner Bros., The Walt Disney Company, NBC Universal, Nickelodeon, Cartoon Network, and ABC. In addition to three major studios, Burbank is home to seven hundred media-related companies, including television networks, broadcasting companies, and music labels.

© Disney

Warner Bros. Studios |

A member of the Burbank community for more than eighty years, Warner Bros. Studios is a leader in producing all forms of entertainment for global audiences. Drawing on a legacy of unrivaled creativity, innovation, and diversity of offerings and collaborators, the company stands at the forefront of every

(Clockwise from top left) Harry, Jack, Sam, and Albert Warner founded Warner Bros. in April 1923. Photo courtesy of Warner Bros. Studios.

THE WARNER BROTHERS

Top Left: Construction on the Studio's backlot, circa 1926.

Middle Left: Warner Bros. Studios entrance, circa 1930.

Right: The Warner Bros. payroll department's cashier window was frequented by actors and crew, circa 1939.

Photos courtesy of Warner Bros. Studios.

aspect of the industry, including films, television, home entertainment, video games, original content for digital distribution, animation, product and brand licensing, comic books, international cinemas, and broadcasting. The company's 110-acre main lot and 32-acre Warner Ranch are among the foremost film and television production and post-production facilities in the world and include 35 sound stages, a backlot that serves as outdoor filming areas, and a complete range of production and post-production services.

Since its founding in 1923, Warner Bros. has been synonymous with unparalleled excellence in filmmaking. Many of its early "contract players" went on to shine as some of the greatest stars of all time: Bette Davis, James Cagney, Humphrey Bogart, Edward G. Robinson, and Errol Flynn, among others. And, over the last eight decades, the studio has released hundreds of memorable films such as *The Maltese Falcon, Casablanca, A Streetcar Named Desire, Rebel Without a Cause, The Music Man, My Fair Lady, Bonnie and Clyde, Cool Hand Luke, Dirty Harry, Chariots of Fire, Driving Miss Daisy, Unforgiven, The Matrix* trilogy, *The Dark Knight,* and the *Harry Potter* films, which have become the most successful film franchise in history.

Always a company to embrace technology and innovation, Warner Bros. made its way into television in 1955 with the debut of the western adventure *Cheyenne.* Other now-classic shows, including *Maverick* and *77 Sunset Strip,* paved the way for hits such as *F Troop, Kung Fu, Alice, Murphy Brown, China Beach, Growing Pains, ER, Friends, Smallville, Two and a Half Men,* and *The Big Bang Theory,* as well as the miniseries *Roots, The Thorn Birds,* and *North & South.*

Countless changes have taken place at Warner Bros. throughout the years, but what hasn't changed is the company's commitment to its hometown. Warner Bros. supports Burbank through economic development, philanthropic giving, employee volunteerism, and civic leadership, and continually seeks out new opportunities through which to have a positive impact on the community.

UNFORGIVEN © Warner Bros., a division of Time Warner Entertainment Company, L.P.

Top Right: Aerial photo of Warner Bros.' main lot, 1933.

Middle Right: Clint Eastwood on the set of *Unforgiven,* which received four Academy Awards, including Best Picture and Best Director (Eastwood).

Middle Left: The Studio's Gate 2 on Olive Avenue was featured in Mel Brooks' 1974 film *Blazing Saddles.*

Bottom Right: Warner Bros. Animation's beloved *Looney Tunes*—including Bugs Bunny, Sylvester, Taz, Road Runner, Tweety, Porky Pig, and Daffy Duck—have been featured in countless animated television series, feature films, made-for-video releases, and more.

Photos courtesy of Warner Bros. Studios.

Top Left: A behind-the-scenes look at Humphrey Bogart and Ingrid Bergman on the set of the 1942 classic film *Casablanca.*

Bottom Left: Warner Bros. Studios' New York Street and Embassy Courtyard backlots were transformed into a late-1800s Japanese village for *The Last Samurai,* 2003.

Top Right: The Emmy Award–winning *The Ellen DeGeneres Show,* produced by Warner Bros. Television Group's Telepictures Productions, debuted in 2003.

Middle Right: One of the most popular and successful television shows of all time, *Friends,* produced by Warner Bros. Television, filmed on Warner's Burbank lot for ten seasons.

Photos courtesy of Warner Bros. Studios.

The Walt Disney Studios | *by Dave Smith, Founder, Walt Disney Archives*

Following the worldwide success of Walt and Roy Disney's first full-length animated feature, *Snow White and the Seven Dwarfs,* Walt determined he needed to increase the size of the studio to accommodate its ever-growing staff. In 1938, he made a deposit on a fifty-one-acre plot off Buena Vista Street in Burbank and began to design state-of-the-art facilities to produce animated films.

Walt supervised all facets of the design and construction of the modern studio. In 1939, The Walt Disney Studios moved to the new Burbank location. Walt created a campus-like setting that consisted of an animation building, sound recording stages, industrial shops, theater, commissary, and additional buildings for inking and painting, camera, and editing work.

Pinocchio and *Fantasia* were the first releases from The Walt Disney Studios in Burbank. During the next twenty years, Disney followed with the full-length animated classics *Dumbo, Bambi, Cinderella, Alice in Wonderland, Peter Pan,* and *Sleeping Beauty.*

© Disney

Top: Walt Disney, seen here near The Walt Disney Studios' original Animation Building in the 1940s, was successful in creating a campus-like atmosphere for employees, an environment which continues to inspire workers and visitors today.

Right: Company founder Walt Disney poses with some of his most famous characters at the Buena Vista Street entrance to Burbank's Walt Disney Studios in 1948.

Photos courtesy of The Walt Disney Company.

© Disney

© Disney

In 1946, Disney expanded into live-action features with *Song of the South*. The Walt Disney Music Company released its first record from the animated feature *Cinderella*. New sound stages were later built on the studio lot and used for movies such as *20,000 Leagues Under the Sea, Mary Poppins,* and for the television show *Mickey Mouse Club*.

Company expansion led to many layout changes at The Walt Disney Studios. In 1976, a major office building was completed and named for the company's co-founder, Roy O. Disney. Burbank also became headquarters for Disney Channel, Walt Disney Records, and Walt Disney Home Entertainment. In 1990, construction was completed on the Team Disney Building with administrative offices featuring the statues of the Seven Dwarfs. In 1996, Disney acquired Capital Cities/ABC Inc., which included the ABC television network and cable networks A&E, Lifetime, History Channel, and ESPN. In 2000, ABC moved into their new building in Burbank.

Top: The Walt Disney Studios, seen here in 1960, features an iconic, 135'6" water tower that originally held 150,000 gallons of water.

Top Left: On the Studios' sound stages, live models were filmed enacting scenes from animated projects, a process that allowed artists to create realistic movements. Here, English actress Kathryn Beaumont served as the model of Alice, a character she also voiced for the 1951 animated feature *Alice in Wonderland*.

Middle Left: Stage 3 was constructed specifically for filming the 1954 film *20,000 Leagues Under the Sea*. Here, the menacing squid attacks the mighty *Nautilus* in a water tank built for the climactic scene.

Bottom Left: Animation artist and Disney Legend Frank Thomas references a live Dalmatian for bringing Pongo to life in *One Hundred and One Dalmatians*, released in 1961.

Photos courtesy of The Walt Disney Company.

© Disney

© Disney

Top: The Team Disney Building, designed by architect Michael Graves, has been The Walt Disney Company's corporate headquarters at The Walt Disney Studios since 1990.

Bottom: The signpost at the corner of Mickey Avenue and Dopey Drive, a movie prop from 1941's *The Reluctant Dragon*, remains a beloved icon of The Walt Disney Studios.

Photos courtesy of The Walt Disney Company.

Disney has continued to be a leader in entertainment with blockbuster animation releases such as *The Little Mermaid, Beauty and the Beast, Aladdin, The Lion King, Pocahontas,* and *Mulan;* with the acquisition of Pixar to develop and produce the computer-animated feature films, *Toy Story, A Bug's Life, Monsters, Inc.,* and *Finding Nemo;* with live-action features *Pirates of the Caribbean, High School Musical,* and *National Treasure;* and with television shows *Mickey Mouse Clubhouse, Hannah Montana, JONAS, Wizards of Waverly Place,* and *Phineas and Ferb.*

The Walt Disney Company has called Burbank home for more than seventy years and continues to be dedicated to providing innovative, quality entertainment for all members of the family, across America and around the world.

DOPEY DRIVE

MICKEY AVE

ANIMATION

MULTIPLANE

INK & PAINT

INBTWEEN

SPECIAL EFX

LAYOUT DEPT

© Disney

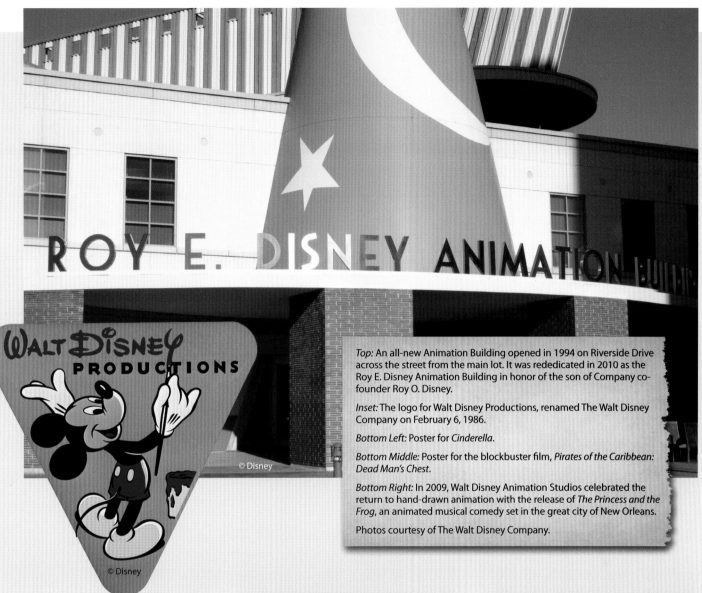

Top: An all-new Animation Building opened in 1994 on Riverside Drive across the street from the main lot. It was rededicated in 2010 as the Roy E. Disney Animation Building in honor of the son of Company co-founder Roy O. Disney.

Inset: The logo for Walt Disney Productions, renamed The Walt Disney Company on February 6, 1986.

Bottom Left: Poster for *Cinderella*.

Bottom Middle: Poster for the blockbuster film, *Pirates of the Caribbean: Dead Man's Chest*.

Bottom Right: In 2009, Walt Disney Animation Studios celebrated the return to hand-drawn animation with the release of *The Princess and the Frog*, an animated musical comedy set in the great city of New Orleans.

Photos courtesy of The Walt Disney Company.

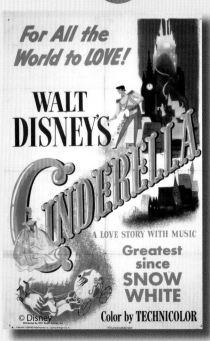

NBC Studios |

In 1952, NBC broke ground for its new television studios on forty acres at the intersection of Alameda and Olive avenues in Burbank. Although NBC's Radio City Studios on Sunset and Vine in Hollywood were the company's West Coast headquarters, the facility was not suited for television. NBC began leasing the El Capitan Theater on Hollywood Boulevard for its Los Angeles–based television productions in 1951, and then moved into the new Burbank Studios in 1952. One of the first broadcasts was the All-Star Revue featuring Rosalind Russell, Milton Berle, Phil Harris, Georgie Jessel, Harpo Marx, Dinah Shore, Red Skelton, and Jimmy Durante.

A few black-and-white programs were broadcast from the new Burbank Studios until the color facility was officially dedicated in 1955. As the first facility built specifically for color television broadcasts, the studio became known as "NBC Color City." The dedication ceremonies included the first color telecast from the West Coast, in a ninety-minute spectacular titled *Entertainment 1955*. The dedication show was hosted

© NBC Universal, Inc.

NBC Studios located at Olive and Alameda avenues. Photo courtesy of Paul W. Bailey, NBCU Photo Bank.

Inset: NBC Studios west coast headquarters opened in Burbank in 1952. Photo courtesy of Gerald Smith, NBCU Photo Bank.

© NBC Universal, Inc.

by Fred Allen with guests Bob Hope, Dinah Shore, Judy Holliday, Ralph Edwards, James Stewart, Helen Hayes, and others.

Throughout the 1960s and 1970s, some of NBC's most memorable news and productions originated from Burbank. In November 1962, NBC's local Los Angeles Channel 4 moved from Hollywood to the Burbank Studios. Upon the move, Channel 4 changed its call letters from KRCA to KNBC. In January 1968, a revolutionary concept in comedy, *Rowan and Martin's Laugh-In*, debuted "from Beautiful Downtown Burbank™." Then, in 1972 *The Tonight Show Starring Johnny Carson* moved from New York City and began broadcasting from Burbank.

© NBC Universal, Inc.

Top: The Tonight Show Starring Johnny Carson. Comedian Bob Hope during an interview with host Johnny Carson, 1980.

Above: Rowan and Martin's Laugh-In. Pictured: (top) Gary Owens; (2nd row, l-r) Dave Madden, Teresa Graves, Goldie Hawn, Arte Johnson, Alan Sues; (3rd row, l-r) Judy Carne, Henry Gibson, Ruth Buzzi, Jo Anne Worley; (bottom row, l-r) host Dan Rowan, host Dick Martin.

Left: Johnny Carson as "Carnac the Magnificent."

Photos courtesy of NBCU Photo Bank.

© NBC Universal, Inc.

In addition to these venerable programs, some of the other shows filmed at NBC's Burbank Studios included *The Dean Martin Show*, *The Flip Wilson Show*, and *Days of Our Lives*. Game shows such as *Truth or Consequences*, *Card Sharks*, and *Hollywood Squares* also originated from Burbank. More recently, the studio hosted *The Tonight Show with Jay Leno*, *Access Hollywood*, and *The Ellen DeGeneres Show*.

NBC has called Burbank its home for the past fifty-eight years and has been a proud member of the community during that time. In 2009, Comcast and General Electric announced a definitive agreement to form a joint venture that will be 51 percent owned by Comcast, 49 percent owned by GE, and managed by Comcast. The joint venture will consist of the NBC Universal businesses and Comcast's cable networks, regional sports networks, certain digital properties, and certain unconsolidated investments. The new NBCU will be well positioned to compete in an increasingly dynamic and competitive media and digital environment.

© NBC Universal, Inc.

Top: The Tonight Show with Jay Leno, Episode 9. Pictured (left to right): Actress Rene Russo during an interview with host Jay Leno in 1992. Photo courtesy of Joey Del Valle, NBCU Photo Bank.

Right: 1988 NBC Burbank Studio tour in front of *The Tonight Show Starring Johnny Carson* Studio. Photo courtesy of Paul Drinkwater, NBCU Photo Bank.

© NBC Universal, Inc.

Top Right: NBC Studios. Photo courtesy of Joey Del Valle, NBCU Photo Bank.

Bottom: Cast from *The Office*, pictured (l-r): Ed Helms, Phyllis Smith, Kate Flannery, Craig Robinson, Paul Lieberstein, Rainn Wilson, Jenna Fischer, Steve Carell, Creed Bratton, John Krasinski, Oscar Nunez, B.J. Novak, Brian Baumgartner, Leslie David Baker, Mindy Kaling, Angela Kinsey. Photo courtesy of Mitchell Haaseth, NBCU Photo Bank.

Cartoon Network |

Cartoon Network Studios (CNS) opened on North Third Street in 2004. This state-of-the-art production facility develops and produces original animated computer graphics (CG) and live-action entertainment exclusively for Cartoon Network (CartoonNetwork.com). Currently seen in more than 97 million U.S. homes and 166 countries around the world, CNS is Turner Broadcasting System, Inc.'s ad-supported cable service, offering the best in original, acquired, and classic entertainment for youth and families. Developed with a "creator-driven, unit-based production model" in mind, CNS seeks to attract the world's next generation of animation talent by cultivating their vision and skill within a custom-designed complex. Housing approximately 235 employees, the studio's three-story structure encompasses roughly 45,000 square feet of production space and 35,000 of office space.

CNS is well known for its popular animated projects such as *Dexter's Laboratory*, *The Powerpuff Girls*, *Johnny Bravo*, *Samurai Jack*, *My Gym Partner's a Monkey*, and *Camp Lazlo*.

CNS takes pride in its extensive community relations program. For the past nine years, the studio has partnered with Robert Louis Stevenson Elementary School in Burbank, creating opportunities for CNS employees to volunteer at the school. Employees mentor students, have reading buddies, lead story hours, and run a Garden Club. The studio also painted and installed a twenty-foot mural for the school's library. In 2010, CNS received California's most prestigious PTA award, the Golden Oak Service Award, given to an organization that has made significant contributions to the welfare of children and youth in a school or community. CNS also supports the mission of Family Service Agency of Burbank, Burbank Temporary Aid Center, the Burbank Community YMCA, and many other key service organizations. This year, CNS leadership also helped create Burbank Shares, a web-based collaborative sharing program between local businesses and the nonprofit community.

Top Left: Ben 10.

Middle Left: Powerpuff Girls.

Right: Burbank Unified School District and Cartoon Network partnership project at Stevenson Elementary School, (left to right) Zita Lefevre, Cartoon Network, and Debbie Ginnetti, Stevenson Elementary School.

Photos courtesy of Cartoon Network.

Landmarks |

Burbank City Hall

275 East Olive Avenue
Year Built: 1943
Listed: National Register of Historic Places, 1996

City Hall was designed and built by George W. Lutzi
and William Allen in 1943. The building is notable for
its Modern/Art Deco architecture, which was popular
in the 1930s and 1940s. The architecture celebrates the
achievements of technology and the taming of nature.

Portal of the Folded Wings

Valhalla Memorial Park
Year Built: 1924
Listed: National Register of Historic Places, 1998

The Portal of the Folded Wings was built in 1924 as the grand entrance to Valhalla Memorial Park. On the fiftieth anniversary of powered flight, December 17, 1953, the Portal was dedicated as a Shrine to Aviation. Twenty-four aviation pioneers are laid to rest in the Portal.

Bob's Big Boy Restaurant

4211 Riverside Drive
Year Built: 1949
Listed: California Point of Historic Interest, 1993

Bob's Big Boy was built in 1949 by local residents Scott Mac-Donald and Ward Albert, and is the oldest-surviving Bob's Big Boy in America. The large monumental sign is an integral part of the building's design and is its most prominent feature. The restaurant was designed by respected architect Wayne McAllister in a transitional design that incorporates 1940s streamline Modern styles while anticipating the free-form 1950s coffee-shop architecture.

U.S. Post Office

125 East Olive Avenue
Year Built: 1937
Listed: National Register of Historic Places, 1985

The post office was built in 1937 in the Spanish architectural style. The location was previously the site of the Burbank Villa Hotel. The interior lobby of the post office is decorated with frescoes depicting early motion picture filming. In 2003, the Post Office was named the Bob Hope Post Office in honor of the late entertainer.

Olive Avenue Rock House

902 East Olive Avenue
Year Built: 1921–23
Listed: Burbank Historic Structure of Merit, 2009

The Rock House was built between 1921 and 1923 and was constructed in the Craftsman style using indigenous river rocks that were likely cultivated from the surrounding landscape, including the nearby Verdugo Mountains. The house was built for and originally owned by Orlando C. Lane, who established a bicycle repair shop in downtown Burbank, later followed by an auto repair garage, and finally a Ford auto dealership.

Sunset Canyon Country Club Gate

Year Built: 1927

The Sunset Canyon Country Club opened in 1921 as a private golf course and country club. In 1927, the Country Club moved into a new clubhouse (now used as a church) and built a new gate at the entrance to the club, which is today the intersection of Sunset Canyon and Country Club drives.

SMITH'S

FOUNTAIN ICE CREAM
CHILI HAMBURGERS SIZE

PORTO'S
BAKERY & CAFE

Compton's
EXPERT SHOE REPAIR
271 EAST ORANGE GROVE AVENUE
BURBANK, CALIFORNIA
BURBANK'S OLDEST AND MOST RELIABLE
SHOE REPAIR SHOP
SERVICE WHILE YOU WAIT
HEELS IN 3 MINUTES
Featuring
O'SULLIVAN'S
AMERICA'S #1
HEEL & SOLE.
Since 1876

MAGNOLIA PARK MARKET
Drugs

Alexander's
LIQUOR   MARKET

Magnolia
P A R K
PARTNERSHIP

Diners, Drive-Ins, and Dives

Trivia and Notable Facts:

The oldest remaining Bob's Big Boy is located on Riverside Drive and was recognized as a California Point of Historical Interest.

Genio Cecchini was born in Italy, came to the United States in 1923, and opened Genio's Restaurant in 1952.

Chef John L. Sullivan created a unique recipe for garlic bread and made the Smoke House the largest purveyor of French bread west of the Mississippi.

Tallyrand got its name from a tasty soup named after the nineteenth-century French statesman Charles Maurice de Talleyrand.

Burbank's Oldest Existing Eateries	Established
Tin Horn Flats	1939
Chili John's	1946
The Smoke House	1946
Bob's Big Boy	1949
Papoo's Hot Dog Show	1949
Santoro's	1956
Coral Café	1957
Tallyrand	1959

Hotels and Motels

BURBANK
MOTOR
LODGE

1025 No. San Fernando Blvd. (U. S. 99)
Burbank, Calif.

COURTYARD

GOLDEN STATE
MOTOR HOTEL
Restaurant
COCKTAILS
ENTERTAINMENT NIGHTLY
DICK MERRISS
TRIO
DANCING

BURBANK HOTEL
DINING AND
COCKTAILS
AIR CONDITIONING-TV

El Rancho
MOTEL
VACANCY
REASONABLE RATES
AIR CONDITIONED
FREE
TV
HEATED POOL

Safari
Inn

Safari
Inn

Airplane flyover. Photo courtesy of
Burbank Historical Society.

Chapter Six

Planes, Trains, and Automobiles

Bob Hope Airport |

Bob Hope Airport began its history as United Airport when it opened on Memorial Day weekend, 1930. An estimated 200,000 people participated in the three days of festivities that marked the official opening. Built by the United Airports Company of California, Ltd., it was said to be the first multimillion-dollar airport in the country, and it quickly became the primary airport for the greater Los Angeles region. While its proximity to Hollywood attracted many movie stars, the airport also drew its share of notable aviators, especially those connected with nearby Lockheed Aircraft Company, such as Amelia Earhart, Charles Lindbergh, Wiley Post, and Roscoe Turner.

Top Left: United Airport, 1934. Photo courtesy of Burbank Historical Society.

Right: United Airport opening in Burbank, Memorial Day, 1930. Photo courtesy of Lockheed Martin.

In 1940, as World War II approached, Lockheed purchased the airport and began expanding its aircraft manufacturing facilities in support of the war effort on land adjacent to the airport's runways. Lockheed changed the airport's name to Lockheed Air Terminal and continued to operate it as a camouflaged commercial airport, even as thousands of B-17s, Hudson bombers, and P-38 fighters rolled off the assembly lines.

After the war, all the major carriers moved to Los Angeles Municipal Airport (LAX), leaving Burbank primarily for military and charter service. But airline service returned to Burbank in a big way when jet airliners capable of using Burbank's runways came along in the late 1960s, and the airport caught on as the most convenient place for a quick flight to the Bay Area.

Lockheed sold the airport in 1978 to a newly formed public agency, the Burbank-Glendale-Pasadena Airport Authority. The mission of the Airport Authority is to provide state-of-the-art regional airport facilities and related services that are efficient, safe, convenient, and user-friendly, while being a good neighbor.

Top: During World War II, elaborate netting was used to camouflage the airport.

Bottom: Passenger check-in, circa 1930.

Photos courtesy of Bob Hope Airport.

Top Left: Burbank-Glendale-Pasadena Airport, circa 1990.

Top Right: Passengers boarding, circa 1930.

Bottom: Lockheed Air Terminal, circa 1946.

Photos courtesy of Bob Hope Airport.

The airport was renamed in honor of legendary entertainer Bob Hope in December 2003. Commercial airlines that service the airport are Alaska Airlines, American Airlines, Delta Connection, JetBlue Airways, United Express, Southwest Airlines, and US Airways. The Burbank Bob Hope Airport is a vital part of the Southern California airport system, serving 4.6 million passengers in 2009 with more than eighty daily non-stop flights.

Top: Southwest Airlines airplane departing Bob Hope Airport, 2010.

Bottom: Burbank-Glendale-Pasadena Airport was renamed in honor of Bob Hope in 2003.

Photos courtesy of Bob Hope Airport.

Planes, Trains, and Automobiles

BATHERS ONLY

Pickwick
RECREATION CENTER
SWIMMING
ICE SKATING
BOWLING
Dine & Dance
SPORTS SHOP
Restaurant

Family entertainment at Pickwick Recreation Center. Photo courtesy of Burbank Historical Society.

Chapter Seven

Arts and Entertainment

Arts

Embrace the Vision
www.burbankarts.com

Burbank, the Media Capital of the World, is a cultural arts destination for all ages. City of Burbank leaders are committed to supporting cultural arts, promoting and providing quality art experiences, access, and venues for every generation.

The City of Burbank established the Burbank Cultural Arts Commission to develop strategies to ensure that the arts are a unifying force in Burbank's urban planning initiatives in the creative economy and build upon Burbank's commitment to the arts education community and its reputation as a media capital.

In 1992, the City of Burbank made a commitment to ensure that visual arts play an essential role in future development and approved the Art in Public Places Ordinance. It required that 1 percent of major construction project costs be allocated towards on-site art, or if desired, be placed in the Public Art Fund, which is utilized to enhance or maintain art located on public land.

Burbank public art:
Top: Perpetual Evolution.
Middle: James Jeffries.
Bottom: He Envisioned Dreams.

Top Left: The Burbank Chorale is the longest continuously performing arts organization in the San Fernando Valley. Since its establishment in 1920, the Burbank Chorale has been inspiring audiences with electrifying performances. Photo courtesy of Burbank Chorale.

Top Right: The Colony Theatre Company is Burbank's premiere professional theatre. It has been named one of "25 Notable U.S. Theatre Companies" by *Encyclopedia Britannica Almanac* and "L.A.'s Best Live Theatre" by the readers of the *L.A. Daily News*. Founded in 1975, the Colony has been in residence since 2000 at Burbank Center Stage and produces a wide range of comedies, dramas, and musicals. This photo was taken from the Colony's production of *Jacques Brel Is Alive and Well and Living in Paris* in 2010, directed by Jon Lawrence Rivera (left to right: Eileen Barnett, Zachary Ford, Jennifer Shelton, and Gregory Franklin). Photo courtesy of Michael Lamont.

Bottom: The Burbank Symphony was founded by Grace Lovejoy in 1922. Although forced into inactivity at the beginning of World War II, the Symphony was quickly revived by Leo Damiani in 1944. The Symphony was renamed Burbank Chamber Orchestra in 1991 and is now known as the Burbank Philharmonic. Under the direction of Steven Kerstein, the Philharmonic continues to enrich the Burbank community with regular free performances, youth outreach activities, and a prestigious annual young artist competition. Photo courtesy of Burbank Philharmonic.

The Art in Public Place Program has made it possible for recognized artists to enhance public spaces throughout the city with sculpture, murals, and environs. The art pieces have become emblematic to Burbank's commitment to the enrichment of the city's cultural and educational identity.

Burbank also has a rich history of supporting performing arts. Several performing arts organizations have partnered to form the Burbank Perform Arts Association to build and strengthen cultural awareness and appreciation for Burbank. Members of the Burbank PerformArts Association present individual productions and outreach programs to entertain, educate, and engage the general populace in all aspects of theatre, music, and dance. Members include the Burbank Chorale (established 1920), Burbank Philharmonic Orchestra, Colony Theatre, Media City Ballet Company, One World Rhythm, Shakespeare at Play, and Victory Theatre.

Entertainment

Loma Theatre opened in 1919.

Victory Theatre opened in 1919.

Sunset Canyon Country Club swimming pool, 1921.

Collins Radio, listening to the World Series, 1926.

Natural bowl amphitheatre (Starlight Bowl) opened in 1935.

San Val Drive-In—located on Winona Avenue and San Fernando Boulevard—opened in 1938.

California Theatre, located on Magnolia Boulevard.

Magnolia Theatre, 1944.

Pickwick Drive-In opened in 1949.

Cornell Theatre on San Fernando Boulevard.

Director, writer, producer Garry Marshall opened the Falcon Theatre in 1997.

Colony Theatre opened in 2000.

AMC 16 in 2003.

Flappers Comedy Club and Restaurant, 2010.

Our future workforce.

Chapter Eight

Embracing Our Future

In order to build neighborhood trust and address vital social equity issues, the City of Burbank anticipated the need to craft a multidimensional outreach program that was purposeful, targeted, and reflective of the realities of focus neighborhood families. In 2005, Connect with Your Community was established. Program objectives were established to aspire to build community and transform focus neighborhoods by fostering partnerships, engaging residents, and inspiring leadership through action.

Connect with Your Community and its partners addressed issues of limited accessibility and engagement through annual neighborhood-strengthening events; workshops in partnership with local nonprofit and business partners; multilingual informational newsletters; a volun-

Top: Holiday in the Park, 2009.

Middle: Taste of Burbank.

Bottom: Be-boppin' in the Park, 2009.

teer program and neighborhood leadership program; and myriad partnership projects that attempt to socially align government and citizen values.

At every dynamic phase, the award-winning Connect with Your Community program quickly became a partnership with residents that incrementally created an environment of open communication, active participation, and meaningful neighborhood change.

Looking to the future, Downtown Burbank has become the commercial heartbeat of the city, offering a shopping destination that attracts more than 10 million visitors a year. The district was hailed by *Sunset Magazine* as "one of Southern California's most appealing urban centers." With its entertainment-industry focus, Downtown Burbank was one of the first districts in the Los Angeles region to offer free Wi-Fi access.

Magnolia Park has become a jazzy neighborhood near the Media District with trendy shops and antique stores. Special functions throughout the year—such as "Be-boppin' in the Park" with its summertime vintage car show, and "Holiday in the Park"—entice foot traffic to the rejuvenated business area.

Burbank implemented a Sustainability Program in 2004 to promote "Green Building" construction practices in both public and private projects that would include both water conservation and energy efficiency. The City of Burbank committed to a "Green" future. Public records, permits, and City business will be conducted digitally. Alternative transportation modes will be explored and city streets may be converted to multi-modal travel corridors with cars, bicycles, pedestrians, and transit vehicles sharing a common space.

The Community Services Building (CSB), completed in 2007, is a significant step in the City's present and future commitment to "Going Green." The energy-efficient

building was constructed with low emissivity, high performance glass, a cool roof, and materials to reduce utility costs. The heart of the building includes an open, central, clear-height atrium that allows substantial natural daylight into the interior and reduces electrical consumption for interior lighting.

Special elements incorporated into the design of the CSB, including LEED® (Leadership in Energy & Environmental Design) components, contribute to the overall savings in the annual operating and maintenance costs for this facility. The U.S. Green Building Council (USGBC) awarded it the gold certification for the design and construction strategy employed in the completion process.

In 2009, the City of Burbank adopted Urban Environmental Accords, which include a series of actions on themes like transportation, parks, and green jobs to further advance sustainability, foster vibrant and healthy economies, promote social equity, and protect the planet's natural systems. The City developed a twenty-second action item unique to Burbank regarding social justice now present in the signed resolution supporting the Accords Declaration and Burbank Sustainability Action Plan. By doing this, the City of Burbank joined other governments in an effort to advance urban sustainability, foster vibrant economies, promote social equity, and protect the planet's natural systems. Together, this effort will help reduce global warming, improve air and water quality, reduce waste, eliminate toxins, preserve open space and natural habitats, create environ-

mentally sound urban areas, and promote healthy communities.

Throughout its history, Burbank has shown itself to be a forward-thinking city. The City will continue to combine twenty-first-century technology with the same small-town feel that has made its high quality of life so attractive. Looking to the future, Burbank will continue to take steps to provide a clean, healthy, and safe environment. The Sustainable Burbank Task Force (SBTF) continues to update and implement the Sustainability Action Plan. Burbank will continue to conduct outreach and educational events including compost and native vegetation workshops, water conservation, Earth Day activities, tours, school programs, and product stewardship.

Youth

In 2008 and 2010, the City of Burbank was named one of the nation's 100 Best Communities for Young People for its effort to provide experiential learning opportunities for young people. This award is a result of quality partnerships and a comprehensive effort to support the success of youth through programs, services, collaborations, volunteer opportunities, and community-wide priorities.

The City of Burbank serves as a model to inspire and educate other communities across the nation to tackle the challenges that face their children and community, and to implement initiatives that will provide them the essential resources they need to succeed in life. Burbank has always had a strong commitment to address the needs of young people who are truly the future of the community.

Embracing Our Future

Community Events

Burbank, 2035

To celebrate National Community Planning Month in October 2010, Burbank fourth-grade students were asked to draw their vision of what Burbank should look like in the year 2035. One winner was selected from each of the eight participating schools based on the thoughtfulness and creativity of their vision of the future Burbank. The eight winners are shown here and provide some insight into how Burbank's young people are embracing the future.

Clockwise from top left:

Ajani Cooper, Stevenson Elementary School

Allison Salvador, St. Francis Xavier

Emerie G. Weiss, William McKinley Elementary School

Fiona Tran, Joaquin Miller Elementary School

Josh Trevizo, Bret Harte Elementary School

Monica Peregrino, George Washington Elementary School

Cheyenne Arroyo, Thomas Edison Elementary School

Christi Zargaryan, Ralph Emerson Elementary School

From the City Manager
[by Michael Flad]

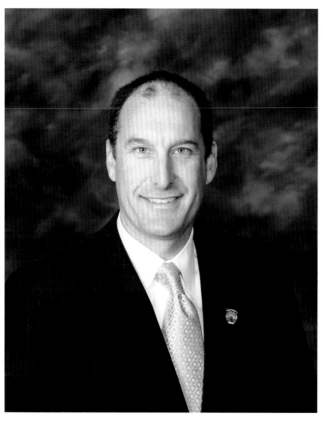

It's the celebration of the century! From sheep ranches and vineyards to an aerospace powerhouse and now the Media Capital of the World, the City of Burbank has successfully evolved and flourished through great successes and tough challenges.

On July 8, 2011, our beloved city officially turns one hundred, and this limited-edition centennial book has been created to celebrate Burbank's rich history. It is hoped that these pages provide you with a glimpse of the traditions that "people, pride and progress" have helped Burbank become the model city it is today.

It's been said time and time again that Burbank is a community like no other. Whether the discussion is cutting-edge aircraft innovation, award-winning motion picture and television programming, or revolutionary changes in the animation industry, Burbank has played an integral part in the world of business. Yet, despite being in the middle of the Los Angeles Metropolitan area, we offer a quality of life and small-town charm enviable to most cities. For those who live or work here, it's the city's reliable services, retail, recreation, and entertainment options that all combine to make it a destination and a place we call "home."

Throughout this year, the community will experience one hundred and more ways to recognize this milestone

as all of Burbank joins together for events and community celebrations. These will be opportunities to reflect on what has made Burbank so special, but perhaps more importantly, a time to begin creating a legacy for the next one hundred years.

When we think about the future of Burbank, it is perhaps best observed in the faces of our young people. As the City, School District, non-profits, and community continue working together to invest in our youth, we ensure their success and the continued success of our community.

From leading the way in sustainability to maintaining the high quality of our parks and infrastructure, Burbank is poised to enter its second century with purpose and principle. The steps we are taking now will lead us to a continued environment of internationally valued employment opportunities, thriving retail, and fun entertainment for the whole family. While downturns in the economy have affected us all, Burbank remains resilient, financially strong, and focused on the future. As always, the creative, industrious, and passionate people of Burbank maintain their indomitable spirit.

As a child growing up in Burbank, I vividly remember the poor air quality, ground-water contamination, and noise pollution issues that Burbank residents had to face. While we all appreciate the strides the City has made to dramatically improve our environment, the vision of an even cleaner and brighter Burbank is being planned by local leaders. From our "green" buildings and our commitment to reduce, reuse, and recycle, to our commitment to dramatically improved transit solutions and the development of green technologies, Burbank is on the forefront of sustainable living. Our neighborhoods are also now more sustainable and walkable than

Top: Burbank City Hall.
Bottom: Mural in City Hall, by artist Hugo Ballin.

ever as people spend more time walking or biking to their destinations in Burbank than driving.

On behalf of the City Council and City staff, we commit to being forward thinking, transparent, and socially, economically, and environmentally responsible in each and every decision we make. The partnerships and programs fostered throughout Burbank's first one hundred years will be essential to Burbank's continued success over the next one hundred years.

As the leaders of today, it is critical that we continue to protect and improve that which was here before us, for the benefit and enjoyment of those who come after us. The future success of Burbank will require the dedication and commitment of not only those individuals who have been placed in positions of authority, but also the leadership of Burbank's countless community partners. For it is the leaders of our neighborhoods, service clubs, religious organizations, professional and social associations, businesses and non-profit organizations that have made Burbank what it is today and will shape what we become during the next one hundred years.

Happy Birthday and congratulations to Burbank on one hundred years of making a difference!

Top: Burbank Gateway.

Middle: DeBell Club House, dedicated in 2009.

Bottom: Alternate fueling station using CNG.

Bibliography

Jenny Aiavolasiti, email message to Gwen Indermill, September 16, 2010.

Bellarmine Jefferson High School, "History," http://www.bell-jeff.net/about/history.jsp.

Bob Hope Airport, "History," http://www.burbankairport.com/airportauthority/about-airport/history.html.

Bob's Big Boy, "History-Beginnings," http://www.bobs.net/history/opening.

Burbank, "Burbank History," http://www.ci.burbank.ca.us/index.aspx?page=43.

Burbank, California State University, Northridge Oviatt Library Digital Archives, http://digital-library.csun.edu/.

Burbank, "A Thumbnail Sketch of Burbank" (City of Burbank, 2010).

Burbank's City Clerk's Office, "Historical Facts" (City of Burbank, 2010).

Burbank Branch Security Trust and Savings Bank, *Ranchos De Los Santos: The Story of Burbank* (Burbank: Security Trust and Savings Bank, 1927).

Burbank City Hall, "50th Anniversary Celebration Program" (Burbank: City of Burbank, 1993).

Burbank Chamber of Commerce, "Advocacy," http://burbankchamber.org/html/advocacy.asp.

Burbank City Federal Credit Union, "The History of Burbank City Federal Credit Union," https://www.burbankcity.org/index.php?content=history.

Burbank.com, "Early History of Burbank," http://www.burbank.com/channel/History/1593.

Burbank High School, "The Blue and White Wave High," 2008 Centennial Edition.

Burbank Historical Society, "A Bit of History," http://www.burbankhistoricalsoc.com/history.htm.

Burbank Unified School District, "A History of Burbank" (Burbank, 1967).

Burbankia History, http://wesclark.com/burbank/history.html.

California Redevelopment Association, "Community Redevelopment Downtown Burbank," http://www.calredevelop.org/AM/Template.cfm?Section=Home&TEMPLATE=/CM/ContentDisplay.cfm&CONTENTID=3747.

Alec Cumming, NBC Historical Timeline, National Broadcasting Company, 2002.

Joel Fox, "Proposition 13: A Look Back, Howard Jarvis Taxpayers Association, May 10, 2006," http://www.hjta.org/propositions/proposition-13/proposition-13-look-back.

Erik Friedl, director, *The History of Lockheed*, DVD (Burbank: Lockheed Martin, 1991).

Full O' Life, "About Full O' Life," http://www.fullolife.com/fifty.html.

Galvin Preservation Reports, City of Burbank, Citywide Historic Context Report (September 2009).

Heather Hall, email message to Gwen Indermill, September 15, 2010.

John C. Hawkins, *This Date in Baltimore Orioles and St. Louis Browns History* (New York: Stein and Day, 1983).

"History of the Burbank City Credit Union," https://www.burbankcity.org/index.php?content=history.

"Hollywood Black Friday: Strike," Serving History, http://www.servinghistory.com/topics/Hollywood_Black_Friday::sub::Strike.

Clint Howard, email message to Gwen Indermill, September 15, 2010.

John Burroughs High School Hall of Fame, http://teachers.yourhomework.com/eurioste/halloffame.htm.

Leadership Burbank, "About Leadership Burbank," http://leadershipburbank.org/joomla/index.php/about.

Jackson Mayers, *Burbank History* (Burbank: James W. Anderson, 1975).

J. H. McCambridge, "Burbank's Power Story," *The American Story*, 1947.

George Lynn Monroe, *Burbank Community Book* (Burbank: A.H. Cawston, 1944).

Office of Historic Preservation, State of California, http://ohp.parks.ca.gov/listed_resources/default.asp?num=P779.

Official California Legislative Information, State of California, http://www.leginfo.ca.gov/.

E. Caswell Perry, *Burbank: An Illustrated History* (Northridge: Windsor Publications, Inc., 1987).

Bruce Petty, "The Southern Burbank Branch, 1981" Los Angeles River Railroads, http://lariverrailroads.com/branch.html.

"School History," Providence High School, http://providencehigh.org/history.jsp.

The Smoke House, "Legacy," http://smokehouse1946.com/smokehouse_legacy.html.

"The Story of Burbank from Her Eventful Pioneer Days" (Burbank: The Magnolia Park Chamber of Commerce, 1954).

Mary Jane Strickland and Theodore X. Garcia, *A History of Burbank: A Special Place in History* (Burbank: Burbank Historical Society, 2000).

Tallyrand History, Tallyrand, http://thetallyrand.com/.

The Walt Disney Company, "Company History," http://corporate.disney.go.com/corporate/complete_history_1.html.

Warner Bros. Pictures, *Seventy-Five Years of Entertaining the World* (Burbank: Warner Bros. Distributing, a Time Warner Entertainment Company, 1997).

William Strauss and Neil Howe, *Generations* (New York: Quill, 1991).

Herb Vincent, Bob's Big Boy Timeline, email message to Gwen Indermill, July 27, 2010.